Unconventional
Chain Mail Jewelry

Textured Metal | Dyed Leather | Beads | Wire

Laura Poplin

KB
KALMBACH BOOKS

Kalmbach Books

21027 Crossroads Circle
Waukesha, Wisconsin 53186
www.Kalmbach.com/Books

Published in 2012
16 15 14 13 12   1 2 3 4 5

Manufactured in the United States of America

ISBN: 978-0-87116-433-9

Editor: *Mary Wohlgemuth*
Art Director: *Lisa Bergman*
Technical Editors: *Theresa Abelew, Hazel Wheaton*
Illustrator: *Kellie Jaeger*
Photographers: *James Forbes, William Zuback*

Library of Congress Cataloging-in-Publication Data

Poplin, Laura.
   Unconventional chain mail jewelry : textured metal, dyed leather, beads, wire / Laura Poplin.

   p. : ill. (chiefly col.) ; cm.

   ISBN: 978-0-87116-433-9

   1. Chains (Jewelry)–Handbooks, manuals, etc. 2. Metal-work–Handbooks, manuals, etc. 3. Wire jewelry–Handbooks, manuals, etc. 4. Jewelry making–Handbooks, manuals, etc. 5. Beadwork–Handbooks, manuals, etc. I. Title.

TT212 .P66 2012
745.594/2

For my son, Keith Burrows, and my grandson, Clayton. I love you very much!

Enchaînements is a French word meaning a linking of scenes or a series of events or ideas, and it is the name of my jewelry business. To me, it's also a one-word summary of how life works and of my journey from a weekend hobbyist to professional jewelry artist. Every day, I create work that I am passionate about. When a person has a passion for her or his art, the "enchaînements" approach seems to ensure that tools, skills, and supportive people will appear on the scene, one way or another.
—Laura Poplin

INTRODUCTION

Chain mail continues to gain popularity among jewelry makers, with its intricate weaves and endless design possibilities. In this book, you'll learn my techniques for incorporating other materials—leather, metal, beads, and wire—into traditional chain mail to produce a hybrid style I call *Unconventional Chain Mail Jewelry*.

This necklace was inspired by Claude Monet's "Waterlilies" painting, which hangs at the Dayton Art Institute. I cut up an image that was painted on leather by my friend Loretta Puncer. I positioned the pieces to engage the viewer's interest.

In the projects that follow, you'll discover endless design possibilities as you begin incorporating the techniques we'll explore together. Sometimes the focus is the chain mail, with a little something extra. Sometimes leather or textured sheet metal takes center stage, and chain mail plays a supporting role.

Each of the techniques I use is not unconventional on its own, but when it's combined with the patterns of chain mail, you can create unexpected and appealing designs. It's unusual to see chain mail on a leather cuff, for example, or hung from a textured sheet-metal shape, or connected with colorful leather pieces in a dramatic necklace. Mixed metals are sometimes used in chain mail, but in these projects, we'll push beyond the commonplace. You'll find some projects that incorporate beads in unusual ways as well.

Perhaps you're already interested in chain mail. This book will help you add new textures and colors to your chain mail work. Or maybe you're a beader or wireworker, ready to step into the world of chain mail. Whatever your interest or skill level, this book will help you pull together layered looks full of personality and handcrafted style.

An organization system made of metal helps me keep my favorite tools within easy reach. Labeled screw-top containers hold jump rings; magnets on the bottom of the containers keep them attached to the board and in view.

HOW TO USE THIS BOOK

The book is organized so that regardless of your experience, you can easily find the information you need. The Basics section that follows includes information about the materials, tools, and skills you'll need, covering fundamental chain mail, metalwork, wirework, and leatherwork techniques. Any of these projects can be completed with the basic setups of tools and supplies explained here.

Projects are grouped into sections that focus on the chain mail weave they have in common. At the start of each project section, you'll find a brief tutorial that teaches the pattern for each weave. Because each weave is best created with certain ring sizes and ratios, each tutorial includes a chart with ring size information in millimeters. (You'll find conversion charts showing millimeter-to-inch comparisons on p. 16–17.)

I suggest you read all the instructions before beginning a project. Use the reference material up front to guide you as you make the project; basic metalwork, wirework, or leatherwork

instructions are not detailed within each project. The required metal or leather shapes will be included in the supply list, with specifics noted when necessary—so use the templates provided to make those items before you begin the project.

As you study a design, imagine how you could change it to make it your own. If long earrings are not your style, redesign them to be shorter.

Play with color, incorporate your style of beads, or change the shapes. Use the elements that you love!

At the end of the sections, you'll see photos of some of my other work made with the featured weave to get you started thinking in new directions.

The Basics

CHAIN MAIL BASICS

A Short History of Chain Mail

Traditional chain mail is a type of armor consisting of rings linked together to form a mesh or fabric-like sheet. Approximately 1,000 known chain mail weaves have been cataloged, and new weaves are invented all the time. Most new weaves have some relation to an ancient weave. A great source for learning about conventional chain mail is the Mail Artisans International League website at mailartisans.org. This is an international archive and community that promotes the art of chain mail.

Chain mail may have been embellished for centuries, possibly since the first armor was constructed in 400 B.C. Research shows that solid metal suits of armor were greatly embellished to distinguish kings and other wealthy and powerful men. Although very few ancient relics of chain mail suits have been found, could the same have been true of mail armor?

Today most chain mail is made into jewelry, although many other clever objects are created, such as sculpture, baskets, purses, curtains, and armor used for reenactments.

This antique chain mail of Eastern origin features riveted metal sections. Photo: Samurai Antique World

My first chain mail bracelet, made with Byzantine weave and a turquoise bead.

Chain Mail Materials

A metalsmith friend and I were discussing how people abuse jewelry and expect it to last forever when they wear it every day. When she said to me, "Jewelry is body adornment, not body armor," I laughed, because the jewelry I make—chain mail—is meant to be armor. Some people are harder on their jewelry than others. When I make something, I assume the worst and make my jewelry as sturdy as possible. The temper (hardness), wire gauge (thickness), and ring size all determine the strength of your chain mail, so consider all of these factors as you choose your rings.

Handmade copper jump rings

RING TYPES

Most chain mail weaves require specific wire gauges and ring sizes, so pay attention to these specifications when ordering jump rings from a supplier. There's nothing more frustrating than when the incorrect ring sizes arrive and your project gratification is delayed! Most designs specify the inside diameter (ID) of the rings, so make sure you and your supplier are speaking the same language.

Many of the book projects require sizes not available commercially, so you will want to learn and practice making your own from wire. If you have the ability to make your own jump rings, you'll always have the correct size ring available on short notice. Several ring-cutting setups are sold, such as the Jump Ringer. Some artists wind their wire around a mandrel and cut them using a jeweler's saw. (You'll find instructions for doing this on p. 15.)

METALS

The type and strength of the metal wire used for chain mail are key. These factors are especially important for bracelets, which take more abuse than necklaces or earrings.

Sterling silver consists of 92.5% pure silver and 7.5% copper. Sterling silver tarnishes, so keep that in mind when choosing wire.

Argentium sterling silver consists of 92.5% pure silver and 7.5% germanium, and is tarnish resistant, which is a big benefit to those who love the sparkling look of highly polished silver. The melting point of Argentium sterling silver is 60°F (16°C) lower than traditional sterling silver, which makes soldering a little more difficult unless you are experienced.

Copper is usually sold as a soft metal, although hard copper can be found at some jewelry suppliers. Any size and gauge of copper jump rings will be fine for earrings or a necklace. To anticipate the hard wear a bracelet usually takes, choose thicker gauges or use a weave that distributes the stress points equally, such as European 4-in-1 or Byzantine.

Brass is an alloy of copper and 33% zinc, making the temper harder than copper alone.

Stainless steel is a great replacement for sterling silver. It's much stronger—so much stronger that it will ruin your regular jeweler's pliers. Electrician's

Three of my favorite materials—sterling silver, brass, and copper wire

pliers or other heavy-duty pliers are best for working with stainless. I recommend that you purchase commercially made rings if you want to work with stainless steel.

There are many other types of metals to use in your chain mail designs. My favorites are the first four, and you'll see them used throughout this book.

METAL TEMPER

When purchase wire for making your own jump rings, you'll encounter a temper designation: dead-soft, half-hard, and full-hard are the most common. This refers to the workability of the wire. As you work with metal, it becomes less malleable—this process is called work-hardening.

Many suppliers of finished jump rings don't specify temper; you can assume the jump rings are half-hard, which offers the best balance between workability and strength. As you open and close the rings, they will work-harden further, resulting in a strong piece of jewelry.

Full-hard jump rings will work if your weave calls for opening and closing the rings just a few times. I don't recommend using dead-soft jump rings at all because they will harden only to about half-hard, and the finished chain mail will distort or twist easily.

Chain Mail Tools

The only tools absolutely necessary to make chain mail are two pairs of pliers, although it's helpful to have a strong pair of reading glasses and good lighting. Most of the additional tools you'll need are for making your own jump rings.

CHAIN MAIL/WIREWORK TOOLKIT
- **2 pairs of jewelry pliers**
- **Roundnose pliers**
- **Tray with liner**
- **Wire gauge**
- **Flush cutters**
- **Mandrels and ring-cutting setup (optional—needed only if you're making your own jump rings)**

Flush cutters are best for cutting wire, leaving the ends as smooth as possible with a minimal bur. You'll need **jewelry-grade pliers** with flat, smooth jaws—I suggest you use one chainnose pliers and one flatnose pliers (some people enjoy using bentnose pliers instead). The finely tapered jaws of chainnose pliers are especially helpful if you're using small rings in your design. Add **roundnose pliers**, and you'll have all the tools you'll need for wirework as well.

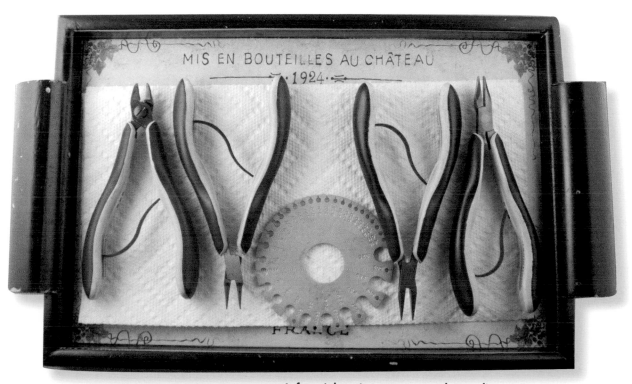

Left to right: wire cutters, roundnose pliers, wire gauge, flatnose pliers, and chainnose pliers on a lined tray

My setup for making and cutting jump rings

A **wire gauge** is useful for confirming wire diameter. Suppliers usually sell wire by gauge, so it's a helpful measure to know.

Use a **small tray with a liner** of a paper towel or pad to keep your rings from spilling. The tray gives you the flexibility to work in front of the TV or even outdoors if you wish. My idea of a most wonderful evening is a tray full of rings, a chick flick on TV (preferably one I've already seen three or four times), and my big Weimaraner, Daisy, sitting next to me.

Many of the projects require ring sizes that aren't readily available, so it's quite handy (not to mention economical) to know how to cut your own rings. Many **ring cutting setups** are available; to decide what's best for you, take into consideration the type of metal you use, and whether you will be a high-capacity user. Most jewelry-grade cutters can't handle cutting stainless steel because the metal is too hard.

I'm still using my first cutting setup, which is very basic. If you like chain mail and making your own rings, you may want to invest in a high-quality setup.

Mandrels for jump rings are available in millimeters and inches, and it's advantageous (but not imperative) to have sets of both styles because some measurements have no precise conversion. (That's why you'll see some measurements in millimeters and others in inches throughout the tutorials and project instructions.) Knitting needles or metal rods from the hardware store can also be used as mandrels.

You can choose among several **cutting methods**—use flush cutters, a jeweler's saw, or a power tool with a trough for holding the rings.

Chain Mail Techniques

WORKING WITH JUMP RINGS

Working with jump rings properly is key if your goal is to make a quality piece of jewelry you will be proud to wear.

How to open and close a jump ring

Hold the jump ring with two pairs of flat-jawed pliers, placing one pliers on either side of the cut in the ring. To open the jump ring, bring one pair of pliers toward you and push the other pair away from you **[A]**. Do not pull the jump ring open sideways.

To close the jump ring, reverse the direction of the pliers to bring the ends of the jump ring back together **[B]**. Because jump rings, especially those used in chain mail, tend to spring back, bring the ends of the ring a bit past the closed position and then bring them back together (you may hear a click as the ends connect).

Repeat several times to work-harden the ring as you close it. Look at the ring from both sides and the top to ensure it's closed perfectly **[C]**.

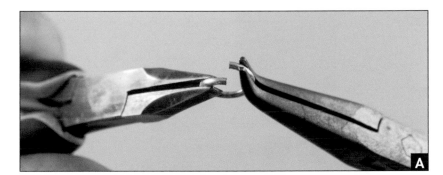

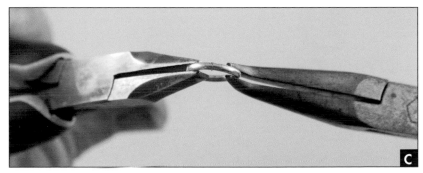

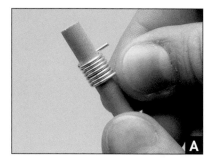

MAKING YOUR OWN JUMP RINGS

Making the coil by hand

Select a wooden dowel or mandrel with a diameter that matches the inside diameter of the jump rings you want to make. Wrap the wire around the mandrel or dowel, keeping the coils tight against one another **[A]**. Cut the wire that anchors the coil. Slide the coil to the end of the dowel to cut the coil into jump rings using a jeweler's saw. Remove the coil from the dowel to use wire cutters or a flex shaft and jump-ring maker.

Cutting jump rings using cutters

Using double-flush cutters is ideal for cutting jump rings from a coil—the cut will not have a bur (sharp point) on either end. If you use flush cutters, one side of the cut will be flush and the other side will have a slight bur. There will be some wire waste if you use flush cutters, so make a few extra coils to make up for the waste.

When cutting a ring from the coil with flush cutters, position the pliers so the bur will be left on the coil side of the cut. Flip the cutters and trim the end of the coil so it is flush. Flip the cutters and repeat for each ring. This ensures that the end of each ring is flush and the rings remain perfectly round.

Using the flush-cut edge of the cutters, trim the straight wire tail from each end of the coil **[A]**.

Slightly separate the first ring from the coil. Use the flush-cut side of the cutters to cut where the wire completes the first ring **[B]**.

Cutting jump rings using a saw

You'll need a bench pin and jeweler's saw for this method (see p. 19–20 for details on sawing supplies and equipment). Brace the dowel against the V notch in the bench pin, and use a jeweler's saw with a 2/0 blade to cut a shallow, vertical slot at the end of the dowel to guide your blade as you cut the coil.

Hold the coil and dowel with your nondominant hand. Lubricate the saw blade and saw through the top of the coil, feeding it toward the slot in the dowel. Be careful not to cut the jump rings in half.

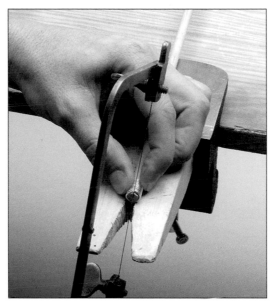

Saw through the top of the coil.

TIP
Place a thin strip of masking tape along one side of the coil to keep the jump rings from falling off.

Using a jump-ring maker and flex shaft

If you have a jump-ring maker such as a Jump Ringer or other setup, the manufacturer provides specific instructions for making a coil, securing it for cutting, and cutting the rings with a flex shaft or other rotary tool. (This is the setup I use, and it's great when you need dozens or hundreds of rings for a project rather than just several rings.)

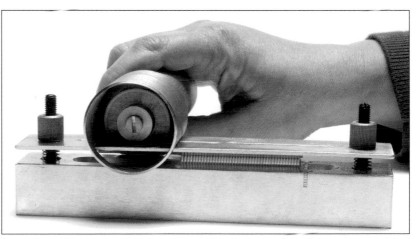

A purchased jump-ring making setup will include a coil holder and a special blade for your flex-shaft handpiece.

Making jump rings

- Wire tries to go back to its original shape when the tension on it is released; this is called spring-back. Spring-back occurs when wire is wrapped around a mandrel and then cut, which causes a jump ring to be a tiny bit larger in diameter than the mandrel. The effects of spring-back are greatest when you're working with hard wire, so take this into consideration and choose a mandrel with a .25–.5mm smaller circumference than the desired inside diameter of your rings.

- To reduce wire waste, cut a few rings and test them by making a sample of the weave. If it works, you can always cut more. If it doesn't, you'll have wasted only a few rings. After you discover your favorite weaves, you won't need to test ring sizes very often.

- Don't try to cut stainless steel until you become experienced with metals, and take safety precautions when you do.

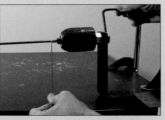

Jump rings will be a tiny bit larger in diameter than the mandrel they were made on.

JUMP RING SIZES

The inside diameter of a jump ring is measured by the size of the mandrel used to make it. Some jump-ring manufacturers use mandrels that are measured in fractional inches (such as ⅛"), while others use mandrels measured in millimeters, which come in quarter-millimeter increments. When choosing jump rings to make a project, this can be confusing. For instance, if the project you're working on calls for ¹⁵⁄₆₄" jump rings and the vendor you're buying from sells them in fractional inches, you're good to go. But what if the ones you're purchasing are measured in millimeters? How do you know what millimeter size rings to buy?

This issue comes up primarily in chain mail projects in which the inside diameter of the jump rings used makes the difference between the project working or not. When you go to buy or make jump rings and find that the measurement system is not the same as what the project calls for, consult the charts on these two pages.

The first chart shows millimeter measurements with decimal inch equivalents in parentheses. The next column shows the closest fractional-inch ring size you'll be able to buy, with the decimal inch equivalent in parentheses.

The second chart shows fractional inch measurements with the millimeter equivalent in parentheses. The next column shows the closest millimeter ring size you'll be able to buy.

*If the substituted size is smaller than the exact equivalent and the design is snug to begin with, the weave may be tight; consider going up a size to compensate.

Ring size in millimeters	Ring size in fractional inches
2.5 mm (0.098 in.)	³⁄₃₂ in. (0.094 in.)
3mm (0.118 in.)	⅛ in. (0.125 in.)
3.25mm (0.130 in.)	⅛ in. (0.125 in.) *
3.5mm (0.138 in.)	⁹⁄₆₄ in. (0.141 in.)
4.0mm (0.157 in.)	⁵⁄₃₂ in. (0.156 in.)
4.75mm (0.187 in.)	³⁄₁₆ in. (0.188 in.)
5.5mm (0.217 in.)	⁷⁄₃₂ in. (0.219 in.)
6.0mm (0.236 in.)	¹⁵⁄₆₄ in. (0.234 in.)
8.75mm (0.344 in.)	¹¹⁄₃₂ in. (0.344 in.)
9.5mm (0.374 in.)	⅜ in. (0.375 in.)
13.0mm (0.512 in.)	½ in. (0.5 in.)

Ring size in fractional inches	Ring size in millimeters
³⁄₃₂ in. (2.4mm)	2.5mm
⅛ in. (3.2mm)	3.25mm
⁹⁄₆₄ in. (3.6mm)	3.5mm *
⁵⁄₃₂ in. (4.0mm)	4.0mm
³⁄₁₆ in. (4.8mm)	4.75mm *
⁷⁄₃₂ in. (5.6mm)	5.5mm *
¹⁵⁄₆₄ in. (6.0mm)	6.0mm
¹¹⁄₃₂ in. (8.7mm)	8.75mm
⅜ in. (9.5mm)	9.5mm
½ in. (13.0mm)	13.0mm

The chart on the right gives conversions of standard wire gauge in the first column to its equivalent diameter in decimal inches and millimeters, which is handy for working with aspect ratio (AR).

ASPECT RATIO

Aspect ratio is the relationship between wire diameter (WD) and the inside diameter (ID) of the ring. Project instructions will always give the ring size for the weave, but sometimes you won't have the exact ring size or would like to make a smaller version of a weave. Learning how to determine AR will expand your design possibilities. So get out your calculator. Let's say you find an interesting weave online and the only information given is that the AR is 4.5. Your wire gauge is .8mm (20-gauge). To get the ring size, use this formula:

WD x AR = ID
.8mm x 4.5mm = 3.6mm

Your mandrel should be as close as possible to 3.6mm or ⅛".

Say you made a chain using 18-gauge (1.02mm), 3.5mm rings and would like to make a petite version of the same chain. Calculate the AR needed for the pattern with this formula:

ID ÷ WD = AR
3.5mm ÷ 1.02mm = 3.4

Now, use that AR to find the ID required for 20-gauge wire. Multiply the thickness in millimeters by the AR (3.4). For 20-gauge wire, the equation would be:

.81mm x 3.4 = 2.75mm ID
(or the closest size to it)

Again, it is important to make some sample rings and try them out before cutting all the rings. Due to spring-back, rings made with hard silver wire will be a tiny bit larger than the mandrel size than the same rings made with soft copper.

Aspect ratio is a challenging concept. Don't feel you have to calculate from scratch all the time; you can make great pieces by following the ring sizes already tested and recommended by other artists. The tutorials in the project sections give my preferred AR for each weave as well as an acceptable range. Jump ring sizes are listed by ID.

Gauge (AWG/B&S)	Inches	Millimeters
12	0.081 in.	2.05mm
13	0.072 in.	1.83mm
14	0.064 in.	1.63mm
15	0.057 in.	1.45mm
16	0.051 in.	1.29mm
17	0.045 in.	1.15mm
18	0.040 in.	1.02mm
19	0.036 in.	0.91mm
20	0.032 in.	0.81mm
21	0.029 in.	0.72mm
22	0.025 in.	0.64mm
23	0.023 in.	0.57mm
24	0.020 in.	0.51mm
25	0.018 in.	0.46mm
26	0.016 in.	0.40mm
27	0.014 in.	0.36mm
28	0.013 in.	0.32mm

METALWORK BASICS

The metalwork skills used in the book projects are very basic, so if you're new to metalwork, don't be afraid to jump right in. Fortunately, the organic look in jewelry—with lots of texture and irregularities—is popular, and many people enjoy wearing a piece that is obviously handcrafted. Practice by using inexpensive base metals. As you perfect your technique, move up to silver.

Most of the projects call for sheet metal in gauges ranging from 24 to 18.

Metalwork Materials

SHEET METAL
Sheet metal comes in various gauges (thicknesses) and tempers. The projects in this book usually call for 18- or 20-gauge sheet metal for a necklace or bracelet; for earrings, I usually suggest a light gauge, such as 24. Most of the projects can be made using any gauge from 24 to 18, depending on availability and your preference. If you plan to add a lot of texture, choose dead-soft sheet metal if it's available. If you prefer to buy sheet metal that's already textured, you'll discover a fantastic range of patterns.

Metalwork Tools

There are countless metalwork tools available and it's easy to accumulate quite a stash, but not all of them have to come from a jewelry supplier. You may find substitutes for some of these tools in your home repair toolbox, so keep your mind open to what you have on hand. Although it's best to purchase the highest quality tool possible, sometimes you can find the perfect tool for the job at a discount tool store or a hardware store—these are good sources for things like mallets and utility hammers, a small grinder, and metal stamps, for example. As you work with your tools, you'll know when you want to trade up.

You'll find a consolidated, itemized list of all the basic metalwork tools you'll need to complete the book projects on p. 24. On the pages that follow, I've broken the list into individual sets of tools for various metalwork tasks.

CUTTING/FILING TOOLS
- **Hand file set**
- **Needle file set**
- **Metal snips or shears**
- **Jeweler's saw and saw blades in sizes 2/0, 4/0, and 6/0**
- **Bench pin**
- **Drill (or rotary tool) and drill bits**
- **Center punch**

Get a set of both **hand files** and **needle files** for smoothing sharp metal edges and wire ends. I suggest purchasing a variety to cover a range of needs: coarse, medium, and fine in flat, half-round, and round profiles in each set.

A pair of basic ($10–15) **metal snips** will cut through thin (up to 22-gauge) sheet metal. If you want to work with thicker metal, buy a pair of heavy-duty **metal shears**.

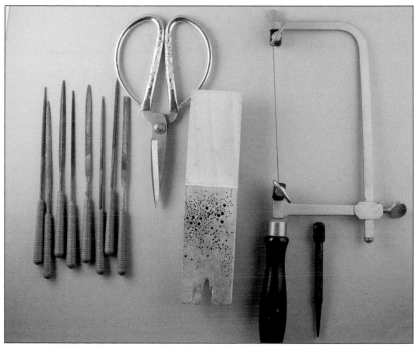

Left to right: hand files, metal shears, bench pin, jeweler's saw, center punch

A **jeweler's saw** is designed so you can easily change and replace the blade. Different blade sizes work with different metal gauges. The chart below is an abbreviated version designed to help you find the correct size quickly. Jewelry suppliers sell blade lubricants such as Bur-Life to prevent the blade from catching and binding in the metal. You can also use beeswax.

A **bench pin** is a small block of wood that usually has some sort of clamp so you can attach it to your bench or table at chest height. A bench pin usually has a V-shaped notch cut into it that helps you position sheet metal shapes for filing, drilling, and sawing.

You'll need a **drill press**, **rotary tool**, or **flex-shaft** to drill holes in sheet metal for jump rings. You'll also drill a hole so you can insert a saw blade into metal when you need to saw out an interior shape (see Drilling/piercing, p. 25). Use a center punch to make a pilot divot before drilling. A rotary tool or flex shaft does a wide range of jobs—in addition to drilling, it will help you polish, grind, de-bur, and even add texture to metal.

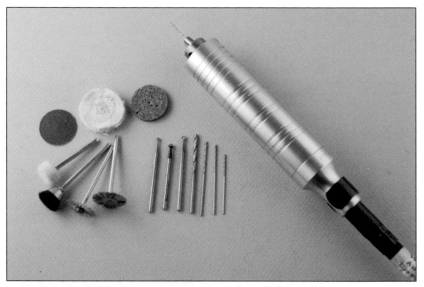

A flex-shaft handpiece with a variety of bits and polishing wheels

Bit	Drills holes for blade size
#75	2/0
#77	4/0
#79	6/0

Metal thickness	Bit range
16-gauge	#58–68
18-gauge	#67–71
20-gauge	#70–75
22-gauge	#73–78
24-gauge	#77–80

Blade	Metal thickness
8/0	Up to 26-gauge
6/0–7/0	24–26-gauge
4/0–5/0	22–24-gauge
3/0	22-gauge
1/0–2/0	20–22-gauge
1–2	18–20-gauge
3–4	16–18-gauge

ANNEALING TOOLS

- **Butane torch**
- **Solderite pad or charcoal block**
- **Bowl of water for quenching**

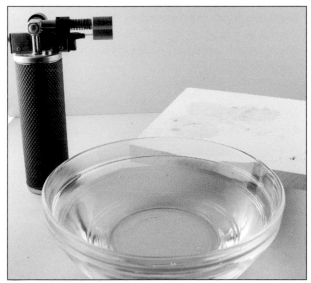

Anneal metals with a handheld butane torch.

SOLDERING TOOLS

- **Soldering pick**
- **Silver solder (wire form, easy)**
- **Flux and fine-tip paintbrush**
- **Pickle and small electric crock pot**
- **Copper tongs**

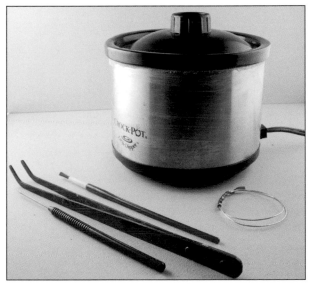

Combine the soldering tools listed above with the annealing tools for a full soldering setup.

A fireproof surface such as a **Solderite pad** or **charcoal block** will protect your tabletop when soldering or firing. A metal, fire-resistant **pick** with a pointed end helps you position solder for soldering.

Use **silver solder** (not hardware store/ lead solder) for these projects. Solder comes in easy, medium, and hard, each with a different melting point for projects that require several soldering operations. You'll need only easy solder for the projects in this book. You also have the option of wire, sheet, or paste solder. I use wire solder for my projects.

Apply **flux** to a piece of clean metal with a fine-tip paintbrush before heating to prevent oxides, which discolor your metal, from forming. Because it keeps the metal clean where it's applied, flux also helps solder flow.

Pickle is an acid that cleans oxides from metal after soldering or finishing by stripping small amounts of copper from the metal. Pickle is generally available in powdered form from jewelry-supply companies. Mix it with water in a small electric crock pot (dedicated to use with pickle); pickle works fastest when heated. Always use copper tongs to transfer metal items in and out of pickle.

Always use **tongs** or heavy-duty pliers to pick up hot items.

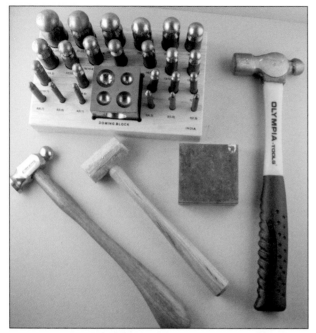

Top: a dapping set. Bottom, left to right: chasing hammer, rawhide mallet, bench block, utility hammer with a textured face

Left to right: bezel, ring, and bracelet mandrels

Disk cutter with dead-blow mallet

FORMING TOOLS

- **Chasing hammer**
- **Texture hammer**
- **Rawhide mallet**
- **Dead-blow mallet**
- **Dapping block and punches**
- **Bench block**
- **Ring, bezel, and oval bracelet mandrels (optional)**
- **Disk cutter (optional)**

Hammers are used to forge (shape) metal. Most often you'll need a **chasing hammer**, which has a spherical face that's good for adding texture, and a flat face that is slightly rounded at its edge for work-hardening and straightening wire. You'll use the **rawhide mallet** when you need to straighten wire or flatten metal without marring it. A **dead-blow mallet** is great for striking steel stamps into metal and using with the disk cutter. A **texture hammer** has designs incised into its faces. Some texture hammers have two different faces or even interchangeable faces.

A **dapping block and punches** are designed for forming sheet metal into domes or dimensional shapes.

The mandrels I use most often, and are needed for several of the projects in this book, are a **bezel mandrel** and an **oval bracelet mandrel**. Other types of mandrels you may find useful are ring or necklace mandrels. Be creative and find a household object to use as a makeshift mandrel; anything that has a sturdy, resistant shape that you can strike with a mallet or hammer will do.

A **disk cutter** is an optional tool. If you use a lot of metal disks in your work, you'll find it handy to punch out perfect disks with a dead-blow hammer or a heavy utility hammer (instead of sawing out the shapes). Most cutters will handle up to 20-gauge sheet metal.

FINISHING TOOLS
- **Sandpaper or sanding pads**
- **Liver of sulfur**
- **Polishing cloth or polishing pads**
- **Rotary tumbler setup (optional)**

Use **sandpaper** for hand-smoothing surfaces and edges. Sanding pads, such as those made by 3M, are an alternative. For jewelry making, keep a range of sandpaper from 180-grit (coarse) to 1200-grit (fine) on hand.

The most common **patina solution** is made from liver of sulfur (LOS), which accelerates the oxidation process on most metals to darken them, giving them the look of age. Other commercial patina products can create colors ranging from bright blues and greens to nearly black.

A **rotary tumbler** has a motorized, revolving barrel. Jump rings or jewelry pieces are put in the barrel along with burnishing compound and media such as stainless steel shot for polishing. (Do not tumble-polish soft gemstones or pearls.)

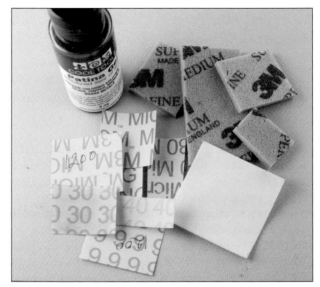

Liver of sulfur solution and a variety of finishing papers and pads

Rotary tumbler

Complete Metalwork Toolkit

Combine the kits mentioned earlier and you'll have everything you need to complete the projects in this book. Here's a complete checklist:

CUTTING/FILING TOOLS
- **Hand file set**
- **Needle file set**
- **Metal snips or shears**
- **Jeweler's saw and saw blades in sizes 2/0, 4/0, and 6/0**
- **Bench pin**
- **Drill (or rotary tool) and drill bits in various sizes**
- **Center punch**

ANNEALING TOOLS
- **Butane torch**
- **Solderite pad or charcoal block**
- **Bowl of water for quenching**

SOLDERING TOOLS
For a full soldering kit, add these items to annealing tools:
- **Soldering pick**
- **Silver solder (wire form, easy)**
- **Flux and fine-tip paintbrush**
- **Pickle and small electric crock pot**
- **Copper tongs**

FORMING TOOLS
- **Chasing hammer**
- **Texture hammer**
- **Rawhide mallet**
- **Dead-blow hammer**
- **Dapping block and punches**
- **Center punch**
- **Bench block**
- **Steel bracelet and bezel mandrels (optional)**
- **Disk cutter (optional)**

FINISHING TOOLS
- **Sandpaper or sanding pads**
- **Liver of sulfur**
- **Polishing cloth or polishing pads**
- **Rotary tumbler (optional)**

Safety basics

Metals
- Wear eye protection at all times while working with metals, wire, and metalsmithing tools.
- Wear a non-flammable apron to protect your clothing.
- Work in a well-ventilated area at all times.
- Tie back long hair and wear close-toed shoes.
- Do not wear clothing or jewelry that might get caught in machinery or catch fire.

All media
- Wear a dust mask while working with materials and tools that generate particulates.

- Read the Material Safety Data Sheet (MSDS) for a new material before use.
- Do not use tools or chemicals in ways that are contrary to the manufacturer's intended purpose.
- Wear protective gloves while handling caustic materials or chemicals.
- Keep a properly rated fire extinguisher and a source of clean water near your workstation.
- Keep cutting tools sharp and all tools and equipment properly maintained.

Metalwork Techniques

Annealing

As you forge or texture metal and feel it's getting difficult to work with, you can anneal and quench it to soften it again. Place the metal on a soldering pad, flux it, and then heat it with a torch. When the metal has a dull, rose-colored glow, it is annealed. Quench the metal in water, and then soak it in pickle to remove any oxides and flux residue.

Sawing

To thread a saw blade, insert the blade, with the teeth of the blade facing down and away from the frame, into the top wing nut of the saw frame, and tighten the wing nut. Brace the handle in the hollow of your shoulder, and apply pressure to the saw frame against your bench pin. Maintaining pressure, insert the bottom of the saw blade into the wing nut closest to the handle, and tighten the wing nut. The blade should be taut and should make a high-pitched "ping" when you pluck it with your thumbnail. If you get a dull "twang" sound, reinstall your blade while pulling pressure on the saw frame. Lubricate the blade with a commercial lubricant or beeswax.

When sawing, sit in an erect posture with the top of your workbench at upper chest level. Slouching or having your work too low causes back and wrist strain and leads to broken saw blades. Grip the saw frame loosely in your hand. Use long, smooth motions, using as much of the blade as possible. The blade will work best when it's perpendicular to the metal. Putting excessive pressure on the saw frame will make you work harder. Turn corners by sawing in place while turning the metal; trying to turn the saw will break the blade.

Drilling/piercing

Whether you're using a drill press or a flex shaft, you'll always need to drill a hole where you plan to add chain mail to a sheet-metal or leather shape. First you'll make a shallow indentation to help position the drill bit for drilling so the drill doesn't travel over the metal or leather and ruin it.

Place the metal on a steel bench block. Tap a center punch with a mallet to create a shallow dimple where you want to drill. Place the metal on a piece of wood and drill a hole, using the dimple as a guide.

To pierce metal, remove one end of the saw blade from the saw frame. Slide the blade through the hole in the metal, then reinsert the blade into the frame, and tighten the wing nut. Saw out the inside section of the metal. Release one end of the blade from the saw frame so you can remove the blade from the metal.

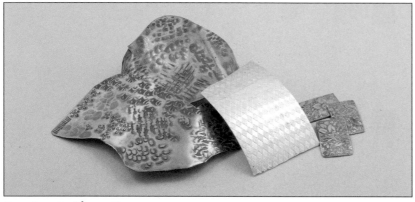

Experiment with creating your own textured metal surfaces.

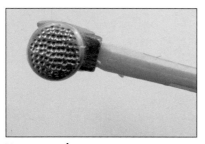

You can make your own texture hammer by drilling into the face of a utility hammer.

It may take some practice to perfect your stamping technique.

Adding texture to sheet metal

An easy way to add texture to metal is to place the metal on a bench block and strike it with a texture hammer. Many commercial styles of texture hammers are available, or you can make your own by cutting or drilling into the face of a hardware-store hammer or by bashing it against concrete. This method creates an organic texture, and you can easily apply it to a large area in a short time.

Additional ideas for adding texture:

- **Lay sheet metal over gravel** and hammer it with a utility hammer
- **Hammer with the rounded face** of a ball peen hammer
- **Hammer a disposable found object** into the sheet metal, such as a leaf, flower, or piece of bark
- **If you have a hammer that's been accidently scratched up**, use it to add texture.

Rolling metal through a jeweler's rolling mill is a professional way to add texture. You may be able to rent jewelry studio time to try working with a rolling mill or take some classes at a community college or university that has a metals studio.

Stamping

Stamping a design, letters, or words into metal is another way to add surface interest. Practice on scraps of metal to perfect your stamping technique. Place the piece of metal on a bench block. Position the stamp over it. Strike the top of the stamp with the hammer. Tilt the stamp a tiny bit to the right and strike again. Repeat, tilting to the top, left, and bottom.

TIP
Use a piece of clear packaging tape over the piece of metal to position it for texturing. Stamp the metal through the tape.

Dapping

Place a disk of metal over the dapping block depression it most closely matches in size. Choose a punch that is slightly smaller than the depression. Set the punch on the disk, and strike the punch with a chasing hammer or mallet until the metal sinks into the depression. Your first blow will make a shallow indentation; each successive blow will carry that indention inward toward the center of the disk.

When the metal conforms completely to the contour of the depression, move it to the next smaller depression in the block and switch to a smaller punch. Form the dome in stages until you have achieved the desired size and shape.

Turn a disk into a half dome by dapping it.

TIP
If you want a hole in your dome, drill it after dapping or you'll distort the hole.

Sanding

To give your metal the desired finish, smooth the surface and/or edges by sanding with progressively finer grits of sandpaper. Begin with a coarse grit (220–400) and work up to a fine grit (600–1000). Rub each grit of sandpaper back and forth in one direction. When you switch to the next finer grit, rub perpendicularly to the previous grit until you can no longer see the marks from the previous grit.

Tumble-polishing

To use a rotary tumbler, place about a pound of steel shot into the tumbler's barrel. Add water to cover the shot and a pinch of burnishing compound. Place the jewelry pieces in the tumbler and seal the barrel. Plug in the tumbler, and let it run for 2–3 hours. Pour the contents of the tumbler into a sieve over a sink, and rinse with cool water. Remove the jewelry and dry it. Dry the shot before storing it.

Using a tumbler polishes and work-hardens jump rings and other jewelry pieces.

Adding color and contrast

In addition to mixing different colors of metal in one chain mail piece, you can experiment with using liver of sulfur or another patina solution to create additional colors. Sometimes I color only some of the rings and leave the rest shiny; occasionally I'll use as many as three distinct colors in one piece.

Using varied colors of jump rings to emphasize the pattern of a weave can add exciting dimension to the piece.

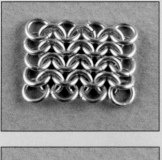

Antiquing with liver of sulfur

After you texture metal in any way, coloring the metal with some kind of patina product can enhance the texture. After adding the patina, you can sand, polish, or use steel wool to restore the shiny metal highlights, leaving darker color in the recesses. If you want to tumble-polish your piece, do it before adding patina to avoid contaminating subsequent tumbler batches with residue from the solution.

Liver of sulfur (LOS) is my patina of choice for copper and silver because it's simple to use and relatively nontoxic. It's available in solid chunks, liquid, or gel. Because of the sulfur, using LOS is a smelly process—use it with good ventilation or outdoors. Add LOS to very hot water for best results. When the piece is the desired color, dip it into cold water to stop the chemical reaction. For a darker patina, continue to dip and rinse the metal.

Dry the piece, and then sand and buff it with a polishing pad or cloth to bring out the texture. It may take a little longer to add patina to Argentium sterling silver.

The usual result of LOS on metal is a darkened, aged look, so I refer to it as **antiquing**. Other commercial patina products, such as those sold under the Jax brand, can produce many other colors, and it's best to preserve them with some kind of clear sealant designed for use on metal. I like to use a water-based acrylic protectant such as Midas Finish Seal lacquer. You can immerse your pieces in the lacquer, or spray or brush on the coating.

The quickest way to give brass an antique look is to anneal and quench it, and then finish using LOS in the manner described above. Several commercial patina products for brass are also available.

Green-blue patina recipe

For a gorgeous (although somewhat fragile) green-blue patina on copper or brass, place the metal on the lid of a large plastic container and cover the metal with salt. Pour ammonia into a small bowl and place it on the lid next to the metal. Use the large container to cover it all, like a dome, for at least 24 hours. When the metal reaches the desired color, remove it and apply a coat of clear lacquer to preserve the finish.

(Dispose of the plastic pieces or reserve them for patina application.) Use this technique only for metal pieces that won't be subject to hard wear; the patina is too fragile for chain mail.

One of my experiments with this patina technique led to the most wonderful blue-green color that reminded me of the Caribbean. As the ammonia evaporated, however, so did the intense blue hue, although the remaining color was very nice too.

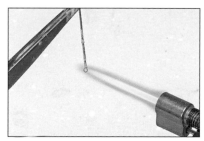

Balling up silver wire to make a headpin

If you're using sterling silver wire, flux the end of the wire that you plan to ball up (no flux is needed for fine silver). Use cross-locking tweezers to grasp the wire at its midpoint, and dip the wire in flux. Hold the wire vertically, and lower one end of the wire into the tip of the inner blue cone of the torch flame. After a ball forms at the end of the wire, remove the flame, and then quench, pickle, rinse, and dry the wire.

Pickling

To make a pickle solution, mix the powder with water according to the manufacturer's instructions. Steel in pickle can cause a chemical reaction that will copper-plate whatever metal you put in the pickle solution. To prevent this, use copper or plastic tongs to place metals in the pickle.

Basic soldering

Although I give you some basic soldering tips here, I suggest you seek out some hands-on instruction on the topic or a good book that's devoted to the subject if you've never soldered before or would like to take your skills further. Practice and experience will help you perfect your soldering technique.

All metal must be clean for solder to flow. Clean the metal by sanding it with 400-grit sandpaper. Surfaces must be in complete contact with each other for solder to flow—solder will not fill holes or gaps. Use flux on all metal to be soldered to prevent oxidation and to help solder flow. Heat the entire piece, not just the solder. Keep the torch moving in a circular motion.

During soldering, the solder will flow to where the heat is the greatest. If your solder is flowing in the wrong direction, adjust the direction of your flame. After the solder flows, quench the piece in water, and place it in a pickle solution (see pickling) to remove oxidation and flux residue. Rinse the piece in clean water.

Exercise: Soldering a Hoop

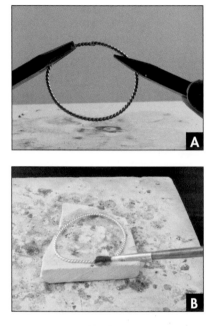

This exercise will demonstrate the basic skill of soldering a sterling silver hoop, which can be used in the Clichy pendant and earrings project, p. 48.

You'll need your metalworking toolkit, flush cutters, file, two pairs of jewelry pliers, sterling silver wire (round or twisted), a large cylinder as a mandrel, and easy solder for silver.

Flush-cut the wire ends and file them if necessary to be sure they will be perfectly flush when closed. Form the hoop around a large cylinder. Clean the hoop by soaking in warm pickle for a few minutes, rinse it with water, and dry. Use two pairs of pliers to close the ring as tightly as possible **[A]**. Apply a small amount of flux to the seam **[B]**.

With the torch, heat a ¹⁄₁₆" piece of solder into a ball, and touch it with the end of the pick to pick it up. Begin to heat the hoop, starting at the point on the hoop opposite the seam and gradually moving to the seam **[C]**. When the flux bubbles up and dissipates, place the solder on the seam. Keep applying heat until the solder flows. Quench the hoop, pickle it, and rinse. Using files and/or sandpaper, smooth the seam.

WIREWORK & BEADING BASICS

When I began making jewelry, I was not very discerning about the beads and findings I collected. Through experience, I learned to purchase only what I truly love. I have the same philosophy about fashion: quality over quantity.

Wirework and Beading Materials

FINDINGS

There are many readymade **clasps** available, such as toggles, magnetic clasps, box clasps, and secure lobster claw clasps. Making your own clasp from wire or metal is an option too.

Although it's fairly easy to make your own **headpins** from wire, purchasing them is quite a time-saver, especially when you're making a piece with many dangling beads. Choose from several types, such as domed, balled, or flat head. Consider the diameter of the wire and the bead size when choosing headpins—make sure the wire will go through the holes of your beads. Some beads, especially pearls, are notorious for having tiny holes.

There are many fabulous **beads** available these days from exceptional artists and exotic locations. A few of my favorites include the organic look of Afghani gemstones, elegant lampworked glass beads, and Herkimer diamonds (a quartz mineral found in Herkimer County, New York). Certain chain mail weaves are perfect for adding beads. I encourage you to use your favorite beads and experiment with different sizes. If you can't find the exact bead shown in a project, consider it an opportunity to personalize the piece—a great benefit of making your own jewelry.

A collection of beads and findings

Wirework

The chainnose and flatnose pliers from your chain mail toolkit will be useful for working wire in many different ways. Add a pair of **roundnose pliers**, and you'll have everything you need for wirework.

CHAIN MAIL/WIREWORK TOOLKIT (see p. 11)
• **2 pairs of jewelry pliers**
• **Roundnose pliers**
• **Tray with liner**
• **Wire gauge**
• **Flush cutters**

You'll use your **flush cutters** for cutting wire from the spool and trimming wire ends after making a wrapped loop over a bead. From time to time you will need the **chasing hammer** and **bench block** from the metalwork kit as well for work-hardening, texturing, or flattening wire.

TIP
Purchase the best quality hand tools you can afford—you won't regret it!

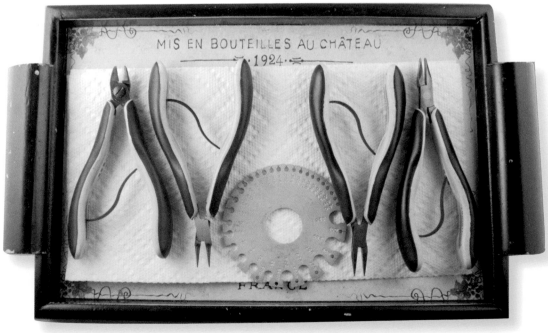

Chain mail and wirework require similar toolkits.

Wirework Techniques

Making an earring wire

Cut two 2" pieces of 20-gauge, round, half-hard, sterling silver wire. For each earring wire: Ball up one end with the torch. Use roundnose pliers to grasp the wire behind the ball and rotate the wire, making a small U-bend **[A]**. Make a second U-bend at the midpoint by wrapping the wire around a ¼" dowel **[B]**. Use roundnose pliers to grasp the wire ¼" (6.5 mm) from the end without the ball, and slightly bend the wire away from the balled end **[C]**.

Place the earring wire on a bench block, and use the flat face of a chasing hammer to work-harden the wire **[D]**. Avoid flattening the portion of the bend that will fit in the ear lobe. Forging the wire will open up the bend a bit; gently squeeze the bend with roundnose pliers to restore its shape. Use 600-grit sandpaper to sand the wire end to a smooth taper. Polish the earring wire with a cloth.

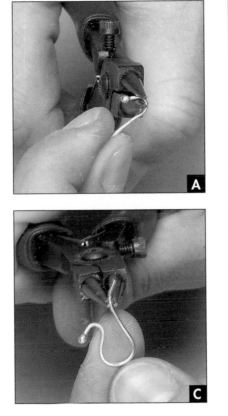

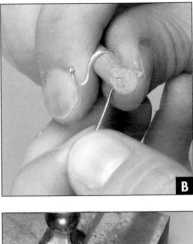

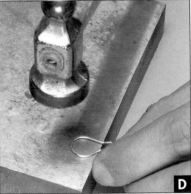

Making a wrapped loop

Trim the wire 1¼" above the object (such as a bead or pearl). Use the tips of your pliers to grasp the wire directly above the object and bend the wire into a right angle **[A]**. Using roundnose pliers, grasp the horizontal portion of the wire near the bend, and then bend the wire over the top jaw of the pliers **[B]**. Reposition the lower jaw of the pliers in this half loop. Curve the wire around the bottom jaw of the pliers. Grasp the loop with chainnose pliers **[C]**. Wrap the tail around the wire stem **[D]**. Trim the excess wire. Use chainnose pliers to press the cut end close to the wrap.

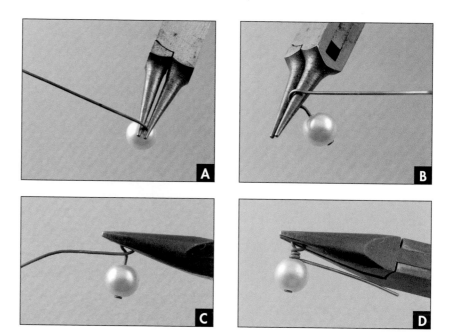

Forming spirals

Grasp the end of a wire with the tips of a pair of roundnose pliers, and rotate the pliers to form a small loop **[A]**. Grasp across the loop with chainnose or flatnose pliers, and use your fingers to guide the wire tail around the loop **[B]**. Continue rotating until the spiral is the desired size. Control the space between rotations to create a loose or tight spiral **[C]**.

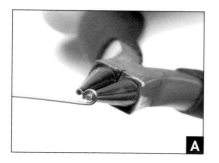

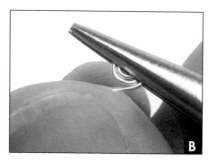

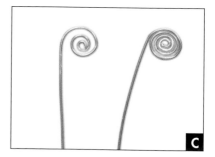

LEATHERWORK BASICS

Leather is a durable and versatile material to work into your jewelry designs. The design possibilities will be endless after you assemble a variety of dye colors and leather! Leather shapes add an unusual and edgy dimension to chain mail.

Leatherwork tools and materials are quite inexpensive, especially when compared with metalwork tools. Note that leather dyes can be a little messy to work with, so be sure to protect your work surfaces and hands. The instructions I share here will equip you with the basic skills needed to complete the projects. There are many other leather techniques, supplies, and tools available. If you become hooked, as I did, you may enjoy exploring more about this craft.

Leatherwork Materials

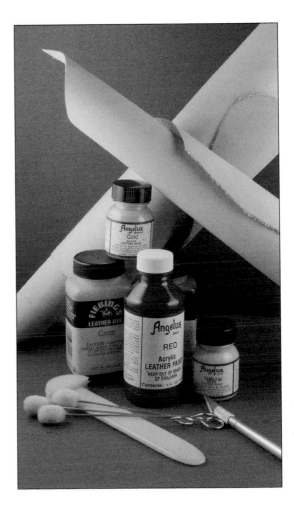

The best type of leather to use for these projects is called full-grain leather, which has no other finishing applied—it's all-natural and will have imperfections. Leather thickness is measured by ounces; one ounce equals ⁷⁄₆₄", although the thickness will vary throughout the entire piece. I usually purchase the thinnest pieces of leather available for my work. Leather usually is sold in a very large piece, so it will last a jewelry maker quite a while.

Consider using leather from old purses, belts, and leather jackets. To refinish used leather, first wipe it down with a leather deglazer to take off the old conditioner. The leather can then be dyed, as long as the new color is darker than the original.

All of the items in the leatherwork toolkit can be purchased at a leather supply store, but many of them you may already own.

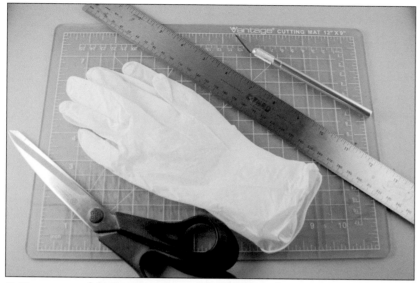

Cutting mat, craft knife, ruler, disposable gloves, and scissors

LEATHERWORK TOOLKIT

- **Cutting mat**
- **Craft knife**
- **Scissors**
- **Metal ruler**
- **Disposable nitrile gloves**
- **Leather dyes and solvent**
- **Leather paint**
- **Wool daubers**
- **Paper towels**
- **Awl**
- **Contact cement and small paintbrush**
- **Leather slicker/edger**
- **Leather balm**
- **Sheepskin**
- **Sandpaper, 400-grit**
- **Wallpaper seam roller**
- **Beeswax**
- **Drill and drill bits (or flex-shaft with drill bit attachment)**
- **Leather antiquing solution (optional)**

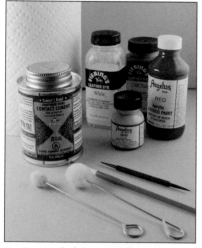

Dyeing and gluing supplies

Finishing and sealing supplies

Protect your table with a **cutting mat** when cutting leather. A good mat is constructed of thick, durable rubber or plastic that is usually self healing. Mats usually have grids for measuring and keeping the piece of leather straight.

Alcohol-based leather dyes penetrate the leather easily and create a uniform color. You can expand the color range by diluting the dye with leather **dye solvent** and mixing your own colors. Use in a well-ventilated room. **Wool daubers** keep lint and fibers from attaching to the leather as you apply dye. A small dauber is best for the small leather pieces required for jewelry.

Leather paint is acrylic paint developed for painting leather or gourds. It's possible to use regular acrylic paint, but it tends to soak into the leather. You will also need **paintbrushes**.

Keep some **basic paper towels** handy for surface protection and cleanup. Buy **heavy-duty paper towels** (available in a hardware store) to apply the leather balm after dyeing.

Use an **awl** for starting or punching holes in leather

Use **contact cement and a small paintbrush** to connect two sides of leather. Don't use rubber cement.

Use a **leather slicker/edger** to smooth and finish the edges of leather pieces.

Use a clear finishing lotion, **leather balm**, before gluing so glue can be removed during the buffing process. Use **sheepskin** for smoothing and buffing leather.

Tips for dyeing leather

Dyeing leather is an art, and no two pieces will look exactly the same. Here are a few hints:

- Dilute alcohol-based leather dye with leather dye solvent to lighten the color.

- Colors can be mixed. Spend some time experimenting with color, and keep in mind that you can always cover a bad color with black.

- To create a rich black, apply navy blue and then black dye.

- Applying dye in straight, even lines will create a very neat finish; applying in a circular motion will create a more organic look. Use some extra leather for experimentation, and learn to love the imperfections you get.

Leatherwork Techniques

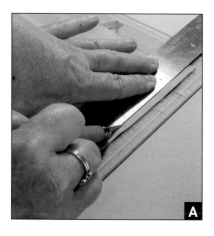

Creating a dyed leather shape for jewelry can be simplified to four steps:
1 Cut the leather to the desired shape and size.
2 Dye the top and sides of the leather.
3 Glue two pieces together to create a matching top and bottom.
4 Finish the edges and buff.

Dye the leather before you glue it. If you've never worked with leather before, experiment with a piece that's larger than the suggested sizes for the projects.

Making leather pieces is a messy process, so it makes sense to prepare a lot of leather at once, even for future projects. Jewelry making usually requires just small pieces, but since they're difficult to handle, it's much easier to figure out what sizes you need, prepare one large piece, cut it to the required size(s), and finish.

Cutting

Place the leather on a cutting mat and trim it to the desired shape with a craft knife **[A]**. If you're making many pieces of the same size, it will save time to make a template out of base metal: Saw or cut the metal to the desired shape and smooth the edges with a file or sandpaper. The measurements marked on most cutting mats will be very helpful for cutting squares or rectangles.

Applying Dye

Cover your work surface with several layers of newspaper. Protect your clothing with an apron or wear something old. Dip a dauber into the dye. Daub a little on some scrap leather to get rid of the excess. Apply dye to the top and edges of the leather **[B]**. Before finishing, you have the option of applying an antiquing solution, which is available in several shades. Experiment on a scrap piece. Use a soft cloth to apply the solution sparingly. With a heavy-duty paper towel, apply a small amount of leather balm to the finished surface to protect it from stray glue.

Gluing

Choose two pieces of leather of similar size. You will glue the undyed sides together. Wearing nitrile gloves, apply a thin coat of leather-grade contact cement to the back of the leather pieces, reaching all the way to the edges [A]. Let the glue dry until tacky. Adhere the pieces back to back. Use a seam roller to roll evenly over the surface [B].

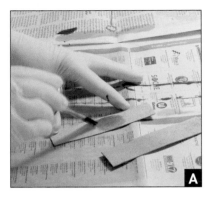 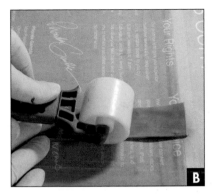

Finishing

It's a good idea to practice this technique on some scrap leather before you try to finish a good piece for your jewelry.

Use a craft knife to trim each corner into a slight curve [A]. Smooth the edges with 400-grit sandpaper. Touch up the edges with dye using a cotton swab or a small dauber [B].

Rub some beeswax on the edge [C]. Run the leather slicker or edger tool along the edges until they're smooth [D]. Buff the edges with sheepskin— first use the rough side and then the smooth side. Make holes by first using an awl to punch the leather and then a drill to finish the hole.

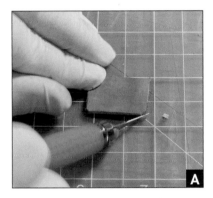 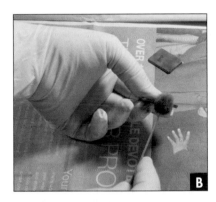
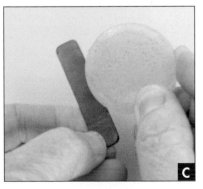 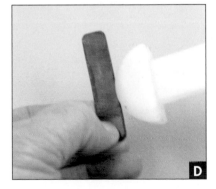

TIP
If a piece of leather is perfectly square, the corners will curl up. Trim each corner to curve it slightly.

Euro 4-in-1
weave

Champs-Elysées

Sainte-Chapelle

Lille

Orleans

Of all the chain mail weaves, European 4-in-1 (which I call Euro 4-in-1) is the most versatile. When made with small rings, it feels like a wonderful fabric. Using larger rings creates a more organic look.

EURO 4-IN-1 TUTORIAL

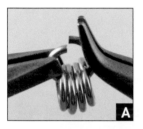

Close two-thirds of your rings and open the other third.

Pass an open ring through four closed rings and close it **[A]**. Place the unit of five as shown **[B]**. Pass a new open ring through the two top rings **[C]**. Add two closed rings to the open ring and close it **[D]**. Arrange the rings you just added to match the pattern set by the first five rings **[E]**. Repeat the previous step until the chain is the desired length **[F]**.

Build a second chain the same size as the first and lay them side by side **[G]**. Join the two 4-in-1 chains by passing an open ring through the inside, top two rings on each chain **[H]**. Continue by connecting the last connected pair with the next unconnected pair **[I]**. Continue connecting the two chains with single rings until the end **[J]**.

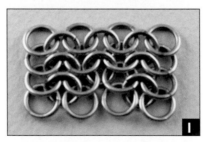

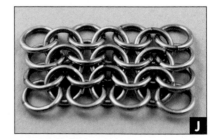

EURO 4-IN-1 TRIANGLE TUTORIAL

Attach an odd number of closed rings to a scrap wire and twist the wire closed **[A]**. (If your project calls for the triangle to end on a wire shape, you can build it on that wire.)

Pass an open ring through the first two rings and close. Pass an open ring through the third and second ring **[B]** and close. Pass an open ring through the fourth and third ring and close. Add one ring at a time in the same way until you reach the end of the row **[C]**.

Repeat the previous step with each row until the last row has only one ring **[D]**. A finished triangle **[E]**.

A

B

C

D

E

European 4-in-1 Weave	
Aspect Ratio 3.3	
16-gauge	4.29mm ID
18-gauge	3.3mm ID
19-gauge	3.04mm ID
20-gauge	2.65mm ID
21-gauge	2.34mm ID

Lyon
earrings

The Lyon earrings feature a textured metal teardrop shape. My teardrops aren't perfect—I like them slightly wonky. You can use any of the texturing methods to create a surface you like; I used a rolling mill for this pattern.

Materials

Sterling silver jump rings:
- 21-gauge ³⁄₃₂" (110)
- 20-gauge 3.5mm sterling silver jump rings (4)

20-gauge sterling silver wire, 5"
24-gauge sterling silver sheet, 1 x 2"
3mm beads or pearls (18)
Silver headpins with balled heads (18)
Pair of sterling silver earring wires

Tools

Chain mail/wirework toolkit
Metalwork toolkits:
- Cutting/filing
- Forming
- Finishing

Sharpie marker
Liver of sulfur solution

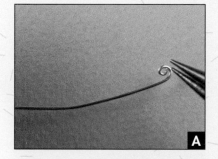

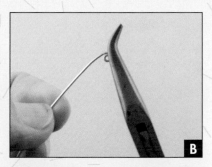

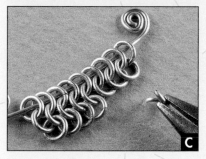

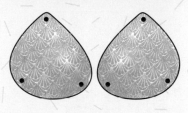

SHEET METAL SHAPES

Cut two teardrop shapes from the silver sheet using the templates. Create the texture of your choice; smooth, antique, and polish the shapes. Drill one hole at the top of each teardrop and two holes at the bottom as shown on the template. Use a dapping block to lightly dome the shapes.

Antique the wire and jump rings, if desired.

CONNECTIONS

Cut the wire into two equal pieces. For each wire: Using roundnose and bentnose or chainnose pliers, make a 1½-rotation spiral at one end **[A–B]**. Using your fingers, create a gentle curve in the wire.

CHAIN MAIL

Slide nine 21-gauge ³⁄₃₂" jump rings onto the curved wire and spiral the other end of the wire. Make a triangle as shown in the Euro 4-in-1 tutorial **[C]**. Repeat for the second earring.

Use two 3.5mm jump rings to attach the curved wires holding the triangles to the metal shapes **[D]**.

BEAD DANGLES

Make wrapped-loop dangles with each headpin and pearl. To attach the dangles, open and close jump rings in the triangles. Attach a dangle to nine outer jump rings in each triangle as shown in the photo at left. Attach the earring wires through the holes on the tops of the teardrop shapes.

templates

Toulouse
earrings

I love to browse flea markets, and I've found a number of treasures for my unconventional jewelry this way. The vintage pearls I used in these earrings are a flea-market find (but freshwater pearls are a good substitute). The leather shapes were a happy accident that was inspired by a piece of silver left over from another project.

My creative eye is always open to interesting shapes in art, architecture, and even scrap metal!

Materials

Sterling silver jump rings
- 20-gauge 4.5mm (28)

2—3mm beads or pearls (28)

Antiqued 24-gauge sterling silver headpins (28)

Leather shapes from template (2)

Pair of earring wires

Tools

Chain mail/wirework toolkit

Leatherwork toolkit

Liver of sulfur solution (optional)

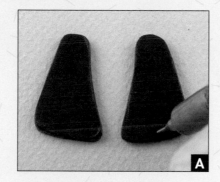

templates

LEATHER SHAPES

Follow the leather tutorial instructions to make and finish two leather pieces from the templates. Make five evenly spaced holes along the bottom edge of each shape and one hole near the top center **[A]**.

CHAIN MAIL CONNECTIONS

Antique the jump rings if desired. Insert a jump ring into each of the five holes at the bottom of each leather shape **[B]**. For each earring, make a triangle beginning with five jump rings as in the Euro 4-in-1 tutorial **[C]**. Place the beads on headpins and attach them to the chain mail triangle with wrapped loops **[D]** (see photo on p. 46 for placement). Attach earring wires through the holes on the top of the leather shapes.

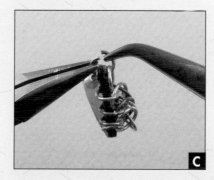

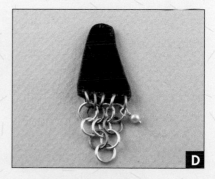

TIP

A jump ring used mainly for connection doesn't need to be a precise size or gauge. Just use one left over from another project!

Clichy
pendant
& earrings

The twisted wire of the Clichy pendant and earrings gives the double hoops extra dimension and provides textural contrast to the shiny Herkimer diamonds and pearls. Create one Clichy component for a pendant or two for earrings—the technique is exactly the same; you'll just change the sizes of the jump rings and beads. If you'd like a petite version of the earrings, try using only one hoop or make the hoops smaller.

Materials—pendant
Sterling silver jump rings:
- 18-gauge 3.5mm (70)
- 18-gauge 3.25mm (10)
- 18-gauge 6mm (4)
- 18-gauge 3mm (8)

Sterling silver twisted wire, 14-gauge, 8¼" cut into a 5¼" and a 3" piece
6mm Herkimer diamond beads (7)
6mm pearls (9)
Antiqued 24-gauge sterling silver headpins (16)
Leather cord necklace

Materials—earrings
Sterling silver jump rings:
- 20-gauge 2.75mm (162)
- 18-gauge 3mm (20)

16-gauge twisted wire, 11", cut into two 5" and two 3" pieces
4mm Herkimer diamond or smoky quartz beads (18)
24-gauge silver headpins (18)
3mm pearls (30)
Pair of earring wires

Tools
Chain mail/wirework toolkit
Metalwork toolkit:
- Soldering
- Finishing

Bezel or ring mandrel
Oval bracelet mandrel
Rawhide mallet

A Herkimer diamond is a somewhat rare quartz crystal with a point at each end. Any clear, faceted gemstone is a good substitute.

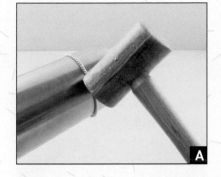

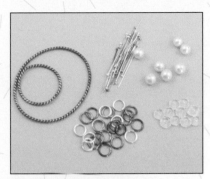

The pendant components

The earring components

HOOP SETS—MAKE TWO FOR EARRINGS
Form each piece of twisted wire into a hoop and solder the ends together. Gently shape the small hoop on a bezel or ring mandrel using a rawhide mallet. Use an oval bracelet mandrel to shape the larger hoop in the same way **[A]**. Antique the hoops, headpins, jump rings, and earring wires; buff the hoops with a polishing cloth or sandpaper to accent the design; and tumble-polish if desired.

CHAIN MAIL AND DANGLES
Working with 3.5mm jump rings for a pendant or 2.75mm jump rings for earrings, attach 10 rings to the small hoop. Add two rows as explained in the Euro 4-in-1 triangle tutorial,

attaching a Herkimer diamond bead dangle to each jump ring in the second row before closing it. Add a ring with a bead on each side. Add 13 jump rings to the large hoop and complete in the same way as the small hoop. On the last row, add a wrapped-loop pearl dangle to each ring before closing it. Add a ring with a pearl dangle on each side of the triangle **[B]**. Make two sets of hoop components for earrings.

CHAIN MAIL BAIL

The bail is based on a variation of the Japanese 12-in-2 weave (see tutorial on p. 98).

For earrings: Using 18-gauge, 3mm (large) and 20-gauge, 2.75mm (small) jump rings, make a 2+2+2+2+2 chain. Connect the end pairs with a pair of small rings to form a triangle **[C, top]**. Make a 2+2+2 chain **[C, bottom]**.

Place the chain triangle above the wire hoop and the straight chain inside it. Use four small jump rings to connect the two chains, enclosing the hoop **[D]**. Attach the small hoop to the bottom of the straight chain using four 20-gauge 2.75mm rings **[E]**. Make a second earring.

For a pendant: Using 18-gauge, 3.25mm and 18-gauge, 3mm jump rings, make two 2+2 chains and connect them to make a square. Attach the bottom of the square to the two hoops using four 3.25mm jump rings. At the top, attach the square to the leather cord using four 6mm jump rings.

Champs-Elysées
earrings

Add a little black dress and the Champs-Elysées earrings will make you long for an evening at a sidewalk cafe. These are definitely special-occasion earrings as shown, but substitute a narrower gauge of wire, and you'll create a more conservative style suitable for work or play.

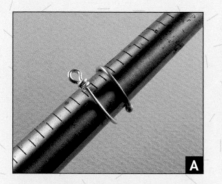

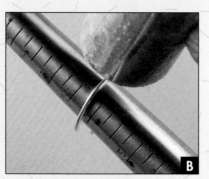

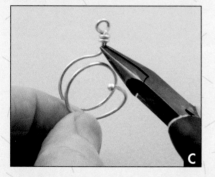

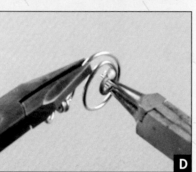

Materials

Sterling silver jump rings:
• 20-gauge 4.5mm (84)
16-gauge fine-silver or sterling silver wire, 8"
4mm chocolate Herkimer diamonds or
   smoky quartz beads (16)
2–3mm turquoise beads (30)
Antiqued 24-gauge silver headpins (46)
Pair of earring wires or post earring findings

Tools

Chain mail/wirework toolkit
Rawhide mallet
Metalwork toolkit:
• Finishing
Butane torch
Ring mandrel

SPIRALS

Cut the wire in half. Using the torch, ball up one end of each piece of wire. Make a wrapped loop on the other end of each wire. Use your fingers to form the first wire around a ring mandrel **[A]**. Strike the wire shape with a rawhide mallet to harden it **[B]**. Use chainnose pliers to make a 90-degree bend in the wire below the wraps **[C]**. Using two pliers, tighten the spiral at the balled end of the wire and make a three-dimensional spiral shape as shown **[D]**. Make a mirror-image spiral shape with the second wire. Antique the spirals and restore the highlights with a polishing pad **[E]**. Antique the jump rings and headpins, if desired.

F

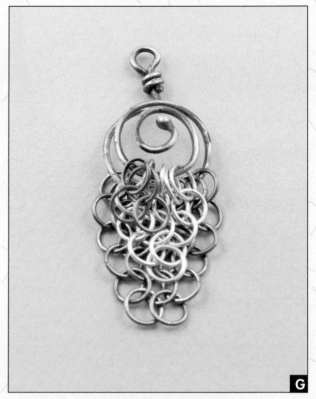

G

CHAIN MAIL

The chain mail in this piece won't look like a typical Euro 4-in-1 weave because the rings are oversized in relation to the wire gauge. Attach seven jump rings to the bottom rung of the first spiral **[F]** and make a Euro 4-in-1 triangle. Add five rings to the next-highest rung of the spiral and make another triangle **[G]**. Repeat to add back and front chain mail triangles to the second spiral.

CONNECTIONS

Place turquoise beads and Herkimer diamonds on headpins. Make wrapped loops to attach them to the jump rings along the edges of the back chain mail triangle and randomly to the front chain mail triangle.

If you'd like to tumble-polish the earrings, wrap a small piece of wire around and through the spiral to keep the mail from detaching from the spiral **[H]**. Attach earring wires or posts to the wrapped loops above the spiral on each earring.

H

Sainte-
Chapelle
pendant

The Sainte-Chapelle pendant started with a vintage medal that I found in a box of family keepsakes. I immediately began thinking about how I could add chain mail to it. The back says, in French: "I am Catholic—In case of an emergency or serious accident, please call a priest."

Supplies

Copper medal or disk
Copper jump rings:
- 20-gauge 2.75mm (42)
- 18-gauge 6mm (12)
- 18-gauge 3.5mm (10)
- 18-gauge 5mm (4)
- 16-gauge 9mm (7)
- 20-gauge copper wire, 2"

Bronze or copper drops (12)
Copper headpins (9)
6mm Herkimer diamond or smoky quartz
    beads (9)
Leather cord necklace

Tools

Chain mail/wirework toolkit
Center punch
Hammer
Liver of sulfur solution (optional)
Drill or flex shaft with #59 drill bit
Sandpaper: 600- to 1200-grit

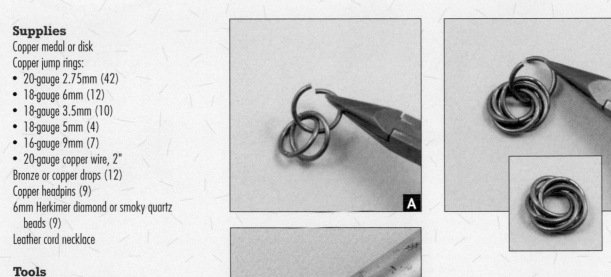

CHAIN MAIL

Antique the jump rings if desired. Pass one 9mm ring through another. Pass a third 9mm ring through the previous two rings **[A]**. Pass a fourth 9mm ring through the previous three. Repeat two more times to create a mobius unit made of six rings **[B]**.

The medal had a great patina already, so all I did was sand the surface lightly to bring out some highlights. If your medal doesn't have a hole in its top, drill one. Drill a hole near the bottom on each side. Make a small spiral on one end of the 2" wire and use your fingers or a mandrel to create a curve in the wire that matches the bottom edge of the medal **[C]**.

Slide on 15 2.75mm jump rings, make a spiral on the other end, and hang
the spiraled wire from the bottom of the medal using two 2.75mm jump rings.
Working off the first five jump rings on the spiraled wire, make a Euro 4-in-1
triangle. Repeat twice to make a total of three Euro 4-in-1 triangles.

CONNECTIONS AND EMBELLISHMENTS

Make wrapped-loop dangles with the Herkimer diamond beads and headpins.
Attach one to the bottom of each chain mail triangle **[D]**. Add another dangle
between each of the three triangles with a 2.75mm ring. Add a dangle to the
spiral wire on each end of the chain mail triangles as well, and one to each of
the rings connecting the spiral wire to the medal, for a total of nine dangles.

Attach the mobius unit to the leather cord with three 18-gauge 6mm rings. Attach
the mobius unit to the top of the medal using a single 9mm jump ring. Add four
3.5mm rings to each side of the mobius unit between the ring attaching it to
the cord and the ring attaching it to the medal. Add two drops to each side of
the mobius unit **[E]**. Add four drops to the cord on either side of the mobius unit,
along with a few extra 3.5mm rings for spacing as shown in the photo on p. 54.

Lille
bracelet

This design combines three of my favorite unconventional materials. It gives you opportunities to express your style if you'd like to vary the colors of the leather and the texture of the metal.

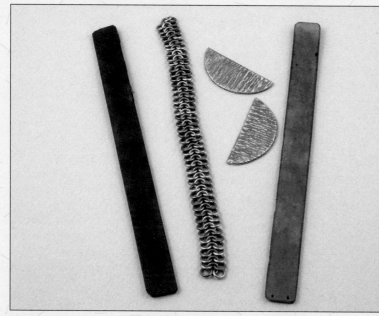

The bracelet components

template

Materials (for a 7¼" bracelet)
Brass jump rings:
- 18-gauge 3.25mm (130)
- 18-gauge 3mm (90)
- 5½" finished leather strips (2)
- Ball-and-socket clasp
- Brass shapes from template (2)

Tools
Chain mail/wirework toolkit
Leatherwork toolkit
Metalwork toolkits:
- Cutting/filing
- Annealing
- Forming
- Finishing

CHAIN MAIL
Anneal half of the brass jump rings to darken them. Make a 5½" single Euro 4-in-1 chain (adjust the length if necessary).

TEXTURED SHEET METAL SHAPES
Apply texture and patina to the metal shapes, and finish as desired. Drill six holes along the straight edge of each shape and one for the clasp attachment as shown on the template.

CONNECTIONS
Place the chain between the leather strips and use the awl to mark placement of 45 holes that will connect the chain to each leather piece. Drill the holes and use 3mm jump rings to connect the chain to the leather. Place a metal shape at one end of the bracelet and mark the hole placement on the leather. Repeat for the second end, marking two holes in each end of each leather strip. Drill the end holes [A]. Use 3mm jump rings to attach the metal shapes to the bracelet; attach two rings to each leather strip and two to the chain [B]. Use 3mm rings to attach half of the clasp at each end.

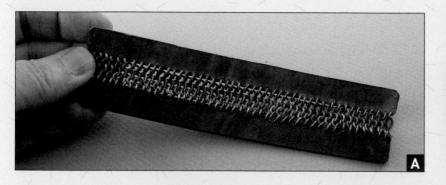

A

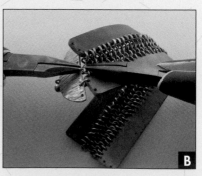

B

Orleans
bracelet

The antique quality of the Orleans bracelet gives the impression of a fabulous European vacation find. It could be transformed into a shiny contemporary piece as well. Texture, stamp, or polish the metal to reflect your individual style.

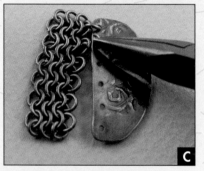

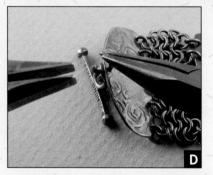

TEXTURED SHAPES

Cut the copper sheet into four rectangles and two half-circle shapes following the templates. Add texture and patina as desired. With a #67 drill bit, drill six evenly spaced holes on both long sides of each rectangle and on the straight sides of the half circles, as shown on the templates. With a #59 drill bit, drill a hole on the curved side for the clasp attachment. Smooth any burs with a file.

CHAIN MAIL

Using 39 2.75mm jump rings, make a Euro 4-in-1 panel three sections wide by four rows high **[A]**. Repeat to make a total of five panels. Lay out the entire bracelet following the main photo, p. 59 **[B]**. Check the length and make adjustments as needed.

CONNECTIONS

Attach a chain mail section to one of the half circles using 2.75mm jump rings **[C]**. Alternating chain mail and metal rectangles, connect the rest of the sections with 2.75mm ring, ending with the second half circle. Add half of the clasp to each bracelet end with a 3mm jump ring **[D]**. The main photo on p. 59 shows a logo charm that I like to attach to my jewelry. If desired, use a 3mm jump ring to attach a charm as you connect the loop end of the toggle clasp.

Materials (for a 7" bracelet)
Copper jump rings:
• 20-gauge 2.75mm (195)
• 20-gauge 2.5mm (90)
• 18-gauge 3mm (7)
20-gauge copper sheet, 1 x 6"
Antiqued copper toggle clasp
Charm or tag (optional)

Tools
Chain mail/wirework toolkit
Metalwork toolkits:
• Finishing
• Cutting/filing

Sizing note: To shorten the bracelet, skip one row of Euro 4-in-1 on each end. If that's not enough, remove another row in the next 4-in-1 section. If you need to lengthen just a tiny bit, add a few extra rings as you connect the clasp. To lengthen substantially, add a row in each section until the bracelet is long enough.

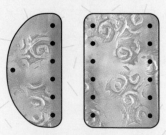

templates

Oops
weave

Autoire

Rouen

Pontoise

This flat weave is often called Unbalanced European 4-in-1, but I like its alternate name: the Oops weave. To position the starter jump rings correctly, you'll need a scrap of strong, flexible material that fits comfortably in your hand. Punch or drill four evenly spaced holes near one end of the material using the template below as a guide for 3.25–3.5mm rings in 18- or 20-gauge, as used in the projects that follow. The tutorial photos show a change in the color of rings for each step to help explain this unusual and somewhat tricky weave.

OOPS TUTORIAL

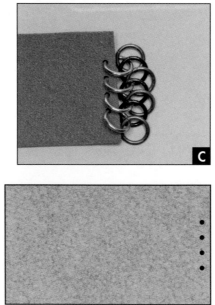

template

Step 1
Column 1: Attach four jump rings (teal) to the starter tool **[A]**. In some cases, these rings remain as part of the weave and sometimes they are not used.

Step 2
Column 2, part a (brown): Starting at the top of the first column, attach a ring through the top two rings. Overlapping the first ring, attach a second ring through the two middle rings in column 1. Attach a third ring through the last two rings in column 1 **[B]**.

Step 3
Column 2, part b (green): Taking care to weave between each of the three rings just added (brown), attach an additional ring to each of the rings in column 1 **[C]**. Note how column 2 is slightly staggered with an alternating pattern of green and brown rings.

Step 4
Column 3 (gold): Starting from the bottom of column 2, attach a ring through the last three rings. Overlapping this ring, attach a second ring through the middle three rings.

Attach a third ring through the top three rings in column 2 **[D]**.

Step 5
Column 4, part a (teal): Weaving between the rings in column 3 (gold), attach a ring (teal) through two of the rings from column 2 (brown and green) **[E]**.

Step 6
Column 4, part b (teal): Above the rings in column 3 (gold), attach a ring (teal) through the two rings from column 2 (brown and green). Below the last ring in column 3 (gold), attach a ring (teal) through the two rings from column 2 (brown and green) **[F]**.

Step 7
Repeat steps 2–6 until you reach the desired length.

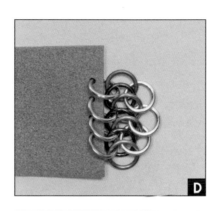

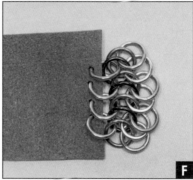

Oops Weave	
Aspect Ratio 3.3	
16-gauge	4.3mm ID
18-gauge	3.3mm ID
19-gauge	3.0mm ID
20-gauge	2.65mm ID
21-gauge	2.34mm ID

Autoire
earrings

Leather gives you the opportunity to introduce gorgeous color like this brilliant blue to chain mail and metal jewelry. If you like drama for your ears, make a pair with two or three leather squares between the chain sections instead of just one.

Materials

Sterling silver jump rings:
- 20-gauge 3.5mm (78)
- 20-gauge 3.0mm (2)

Copper jump rings as placeholders:
- 20-gauge 3.5mm (21)

Finished leather squares ¾ x ¾" (2)
Pair of earring wires or post-back earring findings
13mm sterling silver rondelle beads (10)
Sterling silver headpins (10)

Tools

Chain mail/wirework toolkit
Leatherwork toolkit
Liver of sulfur solution (optional)

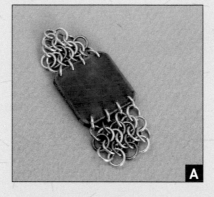

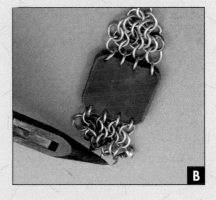

LEATHER SHAPES

Make two ¾" square finished leather squares following the leather tutorial instructions. Drill four evenly spaced holes on two opposite sides of each square (the actual chain can help you determine the exact hole placement on each side).

BEAD DANGLES

Make wrapped-loop dangles with the bead and headpins.

CHAIN MAIL

Antique the rings if desired. Using 20-gauge 3.5mm sterling silver jump rings, you'll create four small squares of Oops weave beginning with four rings in the starter column.

Tops of earrings: Following the Oops tutorial, weave steps 1–6 followed by steps 2–6. Make two of these components. Using 20-gauge 3.0mm rings, attach the four-ring side (column 1) to the top of a leather square. Repeat with the other leather shape. Attach the earring wires or post findings to the tops of the triangles using 3.0mm jump rings. Repeat with the other leather square.

Bottoms of earrings: Following the tutorial, weave steps 1–6 followed by step 2. Make two of these chain components. Using 20-gauge 3.0mm rings, attach the four-ring side (column 1) to the bottom of a leather square **[A]**.

Attach the bead dangles to the bottom three rings and the two outside rings in the row above **[B]**. Repeat with the other leather square.

Rouen
earrings

These earrings take advantage
of the uneven nature of the Oops
weave with a feathery fringe of
bead dangles.

Materials

Sterling silver jump rings:
- 20-gauge 3.25mm (80)

Sterling silver sheet, 22- or 24-gauge, approx.
   2 x 2", for 2 triangle shapes from template
Pair of earring wires
3mm beads (10)
Sterling silver or fine-silver headpins (10)

Tools

Chain mail/wirework toolkit
Metalwork toolkit:
- Finishing tools

Dapping block (optional)

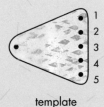

template

TIP
The texture shown is made using a hammer with diamond shapes carved into the face.

STERLING SILVER TRIANGLES

Following the template, cut two triangle shapes from the silver sheet. Add texture and patina, and dome the triangles slightly with the dapping block if desired. Using a #67 drill bit, drill five evenly spaced holes along the bottom edge of each triangle. Drill one hole at the top of each triangle.

CHAIN MAIL

Antique the jump rings if desired. Following the Oops tutorial and beginning with four rings in the starter column, repeat the pattern by weaving steps 1–6, 2–6, and 2 and 3. Remove the starter column of four rings. Repeat to make a second chain component.

CONNECTIONS

Pass a jump ring through the first ring of the Oops weave and through the first hole in the triangle **[A]**. Close the jump ring.

Pass a ring through the first, second, and third ring of the Oops weave and the second hole of the triangle. Close.

Pass a ring through the third, fourth, and fifth rings in the Oops weave and the middle hole of the triangle. Close.

Pass a ring through the fifth, sixth, and seventh rings in the Oops weave and the fourth hole in the triangle. Close.

Pass a ring through the seventh ring in the Oops weave and the fifth hole in the triangle, and close **[B]**.

Repeat to make the second earring connections. Attach the earring wires to the tops of the triangles.

BEAD DANGLES

Attach a wrapped-loop dangle to each ring at the end of a row.

Pontoise
bracelet

The Pontoise bracelet is a playful take on the Orleans bracelet, which uses the more uniform Euro 4-in-1 weave. Although it is uneven in nature, the Oops chain creates a fabric-like effect that feels very comfortable on the wrist.

Oops

Materials for a 7¾" bracelet

Antiqued brass rings:
• 18-gauge 3.25mm (196)
Brass sheet, 20- or 22-gauge, approx. 1 x 6",
   to make 5 shapes following templates
Ball-and-socket clasp

Tools

Chain mail/wirework toolkit
Metalwork toolkit:
• Cutting/filing
• Finishing

make two

make two   make one

templates

A

CHAIN MAIL

Make four sections of Oops weave following the tutorial:
• two sections eight columns wide (weave steps 1–6, 2–6, 2–6, and 2)
• two sections six columns wide (weave steps 1–6 and 2–4).

BRASS TEXTURED SHAPES

Following the templates, cut five shapes from the brass sheet. Add texture and patina if desired. (I gently heated the shapes with a torch to give them a patina.)

CONNECTIONS

Lay out the bracelet **[A]**. Notice that each chain mail section has four rings on one side and three on the other; these correspond to the holes in the metal pieces as shown on the template. Drill the holes as shown on the template and smooth any burs with a file. Attach the end rings of the chain mail to the metal pieces with the remaining 18-gauge, 3.25mm jump rings. Attach half of the clasp to each end with a jump ring.

Gallery
Oops

Byzantine
weave

Perugia

De-Luz

Biarritz

Sometimes called "birdcage weave," Byzantine is a versatile weave. It consists of self-contained links that can be continued in one long chain or used individually. Most often, I use jump rings of equal size and gauge to produce a smooth, uniform Byzantine chain.

BYZANTINE TUTORIAL

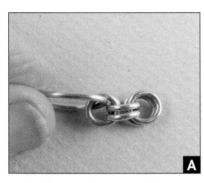

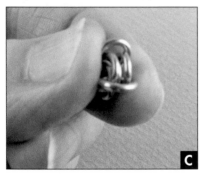

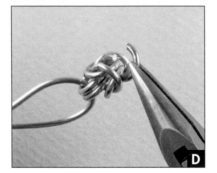

Pass one open jump ring through four closed rings and close. Pass an open ring through the same four rings and close. Lay out the six rings to form a 2+2+2 chain. If desired, insert a small scrap wire through two end rings to make the chain easier to hold [A].

Fold back the two end rings and hold them against the sides [B]. Spread open the two rings now at the end—this will expose the two rings you folded back in the previous step [C]. Pass an open ring through the last pair added and close [D].

Byzantine Weave	
Aspect Ratio 3.5	
16-gauge	4.55mm ID
18-gauge	3.50mm ID
19-gauge	3.22mm ID
20-gauge	2.80mm ID
21-gauge	2.48mm ID

Pass an open ring through the same pair, next to the ring added in D **[E]**.

Pass an open ring through the last pair and add two closed rings **[F]**. Close. Pass another open ring through the same two pairs and close.

Fold back the two end rings and hold them against the sides, and spread open the two rings now at the end. This is the same action you did in B and C. Pass an open ring through the newly exposed rings and close **[G]**. Repeat to add a second ring along the same path.

You now have one Byzantine unit **[H]**. Repeat F and G until the chain is the desired length.

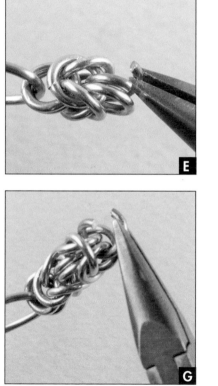

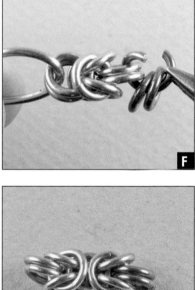

Perugia
earrings & bracelet

The Perugia earrings are quick and fun to make.
The Herkimer diamonds and white pearls provide
a shiny contrast to the antiqued brass. Byzantine
weave plays a supporting role in this design; it adds
depth and creates a base for attaching pearls or
other beads. The bracelet expands the idea to an
8" Byzantine chain. If you like an extra-full look,
simply bring on more pearls!

Byzantine

Materials—earrings
Antiqued brass jump rings:
• 20-gauge 2.75mm (30)
4mm Herkimer diamond rondelles (15 or more)
4mm round pearls (15 or more)
Antiqued brass headpins (30 or more)
Pair of antiqued brass earring wires

Materials for an 8" bracelet
Sterling silver jump rings:
• 18-gauge 3.5mm (184)
• 18-gauge 3.0mm (40 or more)
Assorted beads, 2–4mm (40 or more)
Sterling silver or fine-silver headpins (40 or more)
Sterling silver clasp

Tools
Chain mail/wirework toolkit

The earring components

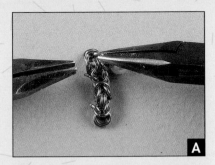

EARRINGS
CHAIN MAIL & DANGLES
Use the 3.5mm jump rings to make two Byzantine chains, each consisting of two Byzantine links about 1½" long. Make 40 or more wrapped-loop dangles using Herkimer diamonds, pearls, and headpins.

CONNECTIONS
Use 20-gauge jump rings to connect dangles to the connector rings—the "eye" in the center of each Byzantine link **[A]**. Attach three dangles to the bottom of the weave with a 20-gauge ring. Fill in any open spots with the remainder of the rings and dangles. Attach the two top empty rings to the earring wire **[B]**. Make sure the dangles are evenly spaced.

BRACELET
The bracelet features pearls, Herkimer diamonds, and various shades of green beads on a Byzantine weave. This weave naturally helps the beads to be arranged just right. The AR for this piece is a little larger than the earrings to create more room for adding beads.

To make the bracelet, start with about 7" of Byzantine chain instead of just two links, as you did for the earrings. When you're finished adding dangles, attach the ring side of the clasp to one end of the chain. On the other, add three or four jump rings for maneuverability, and then attach the toggle half of the clasp.

TIP
Want a longer chain? Per inch, Byzantine uses 30 20-gauge 2.75mm jump rings or 26 18-gauge 3.5mm jump rings.

De-Luz
lariat

This romantic, asymmetrical necklace would look as beautiful with a long flowing beach dress as with tailored business attire. The De-Luz is built off the process for the Perugia earrings and bracelet, with a few key differences. The larger scale requires fewer but larger bead dangles, and the lovely textured-metal toggle turns the Byzantine chain into a lariat-style necklace.

Byzantine

Materials for a 25" lariat
Antiqued brass jump rings:
- 20-gauge 3.0mm (750)
- 18-gauge 3.0mm (20–30)
- 18-gauge 3.5mm (2)

20–30mm baroque pearls (10–15)
15mm pear-shaped crystals (8–12)
Antiqued brass headpins (20–30)
Brass sheet, 16-gauge, 3 x 3"

Tools
Metalwork toolkit:
- Cutting/filing
- Forming

Sandpaper, 600- and 1200-grit

> **TIP**
> To increase the length, you'll need about 30 extra 3.0mm jump rings in 20-gauge (or 26 in 18-gauge) for each inch of chain.

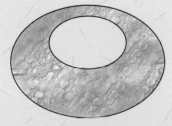

template

The lariat components

CHAIN MAIL
Using the 20-gauge jump rings, make a 25" Byzantine chain.

TOGGLE LOOP
From the brass sheet, saw out, pierce, and finish the toggle loop following the template. Add texture and patina as desired. Use the dapping block to dome the shape slightly.

BEAD AND PEARL DANGLES
Make wrapped-loop dangles with the pearls, crystals, and headpins.

A

CONNECTIONS
Working from one end of the chain for about 12", use the 18-gauge jump rings to connect dangles to the connector rings as shown **[A]**. Use the two 3.5mm jump rings to attach the toggle to the other end of the chain. I placed dangles about every ⅜–½".

To wear, slide the beaded end of the chain through the toggle loop. The beads should drape over the lower part of the toggle.

Biarritz
necklace & bracelet

Experimenting with the leather dye
and paint colors creates endless
possibilities for this colorful set. The
jump rings used in the necklace are
19-gauge, but 18- or 20-gauge will
work as well. Byzantine weave is
superb for adding embellishments;
use jump rings in a finer gauge than
you used in the weave so they pass
through easily.

Byzantine

Materials for a 16" necklace

Argentium sterling silver jump rings, hard:
- 19-gauge, 3mm (576)
- 20-gauge, 3.5mm (64)
- 18-gauge 3mm (6)

Leather shapes, dyed or painted and finished:
- 1 x 1" (6)
- 1 x ¾" (9)
- 1 x ½" (4)

Sterling silver sheet, 20- or 22-gauge, 2 x 6"
Sterling silver clasp

Materials for a 7" bracelet

Argentium sterling silver jump rings, hard:
- 20-gauge, 2.75mm (290)
- 18-gauge, 3.25mm (350)
- 18-gauge, 3mm (30)

Leather shapes, dyed or painted and finished:
- 1 x ½" (8)

Sterling silver clasp

Tools

Chain mail/wirework toolkit
Leatherwork toolkit
Metalwork toolkit:
- Cutting/filing
- Finishing

template

NECKLACE CHAIN MAIL

Using the 3mm jump rings, make a 16" Byzantine chain.

TEXTURED METAL SHAPES

Follow the template to create 11 shapes from the sterling silver sheet. Add texture and patina as desired. Use the dapping block to dome the shapes slightly if desired, and drill holes as shown.

CONNECTIONS

Lay the chain in a straight line and position the leather shapes, taking the colors and sizes into consideration. Use the photo on p. 80 as a guide. Place a half-round metal shape at the end of each column of leather shapes. Check for size and proportion, and rearrange if necessary **[A]**.

Mark the leather for placement of the connecting rings. You'll make two holes to connect each piece to ensure they lie straight. Use 3.5mm jump rings to attach all the leather shapes to each other in columns and the columns to the chain. Use the 18-gauge 3mm rings to attach the clasp.

A

TIP
I recommend using hard wire to make the 3.0mm jump rings used in this Byzantine weave. If your wire or jump rings are only half-hard, go up a size to 3.25mm rings.

TIP
Argentium sterling silver is resistant to tarnish. This set will remain brilliant for a long time without polishing.

The bracelet components

BRACELET
CHAIN MAIL
Using the 20-gauge jump rings, make six 1" Byzantine sections, each consisting of two complete Byzantine links.

LEATHER SHAPES
Make six finished leather shapes, each 1 x ½". Dye or paint and finish. Drill three evenly spaced holes on each long side of the leather rectangles.

CONNECTIONS
Connect a leather piece to a Byzantine section using three 18-gauge 3.0mm rings. Repeat to connect all the leather pieces and Byzantine chains, alternating leather and chain **[A]**, and attach the clasp with 18-gauge 2.75mm rings **[B]**.

TIP
I created the texture on the metal for the necklace using the rounded end of a jewelry hammer. Some of the leather was dyed and some was painted, and I added glitter to some of the leather paint. I antiqued and finished all of the leather pieces.

Chrysanthemum
weave

Chrysanthème

Joie de Vivre

Fleuriste

The Chrysanthemum weave is based on the European 4-in-1, which is one of the oldest, most popular weaves. The units can be attached together to make a bracelet, but unless other elements are supporting and protecting this delicate flower, it can be rather fragile. I like to make this weave using a variety of jump ring colors.

Chrysanthemum Weave Tutorial

The tutorial uses the same size rings as the projects in this section:
- 21-gauge ³⁄₃₂" (55)
- 16-gauge ⁹⁄₃₂" (1)
- 18-gauge ⁵⁄₃₂" (11)
- 21-gauge ⅛" (13)

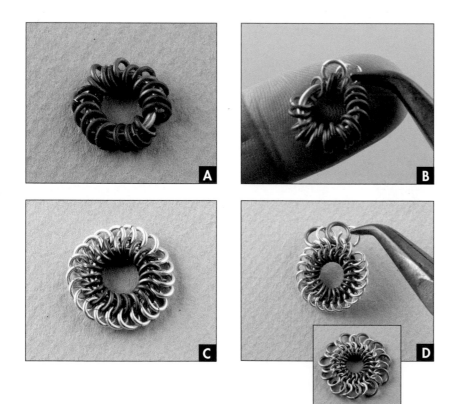

Close 22 21-gauge ³⁄₃₂" rings, slide them onto the 16-gauge 5mm ring, and close the 5mm ring **[A]**. Open the remaining 22 ³⁄₃₂" rings.

Pass an open ³⁄₃₂" ring through the first and second ring, and close it. Pass an open ³⁄₃₂" ring through the second and third ring, and close it **[B]**.

Continue working in the same direction around the large ring, making sure each ring you add lies under the previous ring **[C]**.

You should have 11 18-gauge ⁵⁄₃₂" rings, 11 21-gauge ³⁄₃₂" rings, and 13 21-gauge ⅛" rings remaining. Proceed with the next row in the same manner, except alternate 18-gauge rings and 21-gauge ⅛" rings **[D]**.

Pass an open 21-gauge ³⁄₃₂" ring through two 21-gauge ⅛" rings from the previous row. This takes place in the middle of the 18-gauge rings and causes the flower to become three-dimensional **[E]**. Continue around to create the finished flower **[F]**.

TIP
This weave requires accurate AR. If you're making jump rings, test a few before you cut an entire batch.

Chrysanthème
earrings

The bright green leather leaf shapes show off the mum-like flower of the weave in these earrings.
I like mixing metals in this weave. Consider linking two or more flowers together as an option.

Chrysanthemum

Materials

Copper jump rings:
- 16-gauge 5.0mm (2)

Sterling silver jump rings:
- 21-gauge 3/32" (136)

Brass jump rings:
- 18-gauge 5/32" (22)
- 21-gauge 1/8" (26)

1½ x 3" piece of thin (2-oz.) leather for 4 leather leaves following template

Pair of sterling silver earring wires

Tools

Chain mail/wirework toolkit
Leatherwork toolkit
Tumbling setup (optional)

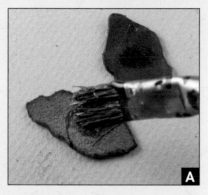

The earring components

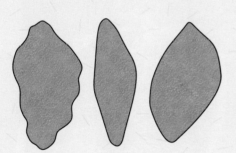

templates

TIP
Use the templates for your leaf shapes—or try using real leaves as patterns. Mix or match shapes as desired.

CHAIN MAIL

Make two Chrysanthemum units following the tutorial on p. 86. Use copper jump rings for the center, silver as the body of the flower, and brass alternating with silver on the outside row. Attach small brass jump rings as the final step to make the flower 3-D. Tumble if desired.

LEATHER SHAPES

Place a leaf template on a thin piece of leather and cut around it with your craft knife. Repeat to make a total of four leaves. Dye the leather and finish, except do not glue the two layers together—thin leaves work best in this design. If desired, lightly sand the edges for natural-looking leaves. Use an awl to scratch veins into the leaves. Using a #59 drill bit, drill a hole near the top edge of each of two leaves. Glue a leaf with a hole onto a leaf without a hole, positioning the leaves so the hole is not blocked **[A]**. Repeat with the other two leaves.

CONNECTIONS

Attach a Chrysanthemum and a leaf pair to each earring wire **[B]**.

Joie de Vivre
pendant

This pendant gives you plenty of opportunities for personalization (hint—it makes a great gift). Incorporate meaningful phrases or add some birthstone crystals or favorite beads.

Chrysanthemum

Materials

For the Chrysanthemum unit:

Copper jump rings:
- 21-gauge ³⁄₃₂" (55)
- 16-gauge ⁹⁄₃₂" (1)

Sterling silver rings:
- 21-gauge ⅛" (13)

For the bail:

18-gauge 3.25mm brass rings (8)

Sterling silver jump rings:
- 20-gauge 2.75mm (8)
- 20-gauge 3.75mm (2)
- 18-gauge ³⁄₁₆" (2)

3.75mm sterling silver jump rings (5)
3 pieces of sheet metal (sterling silver, copper, and brass), 20- or 22-gauge, each approx. 1 x 1½" (enough for 1 leaf shape)
14-gauge half-hard sterling silver wire, 4½"
Leather cord necklace, 16–18"

Tools

Chain mail/wirework toolkit

Metalwork toolkits:
- Soldering
- Cutting/filing
- Finishing

Alphabet and/or design stamps

TIP
Practice stamping your words on a scrap piece of metal to perfect your stamping technique and ensure the word will fit.

The pendant components

CHAIN MAIL

Make one Chrysanthemum unit with the copper, sterling silver, and brass jump rings. Tumble if desired.

WIRE HOOP

Make a hoop from the sterling silver wire, and solder it closed. Sand and finish the join until it is smooth.

CHAIN MAIL BAIL

This bail is made the same way as the bail in the Clichy pendant project (p. 48). Make two 2+2 chains using the 18-gauge 3.25mm brass rings and the 20-gauge 2.75mm silver rings. Lay one chain above the wire hoop and one inside it. Use four 20-gauge, 3.75mm jump rings to connect the two chains, enclosing the hoop. Attach the Chrysanthemum unit to the bottom of the bail with two 21-gauge, ³⁄₃₂" rings **[A]**.

METAL LEAF SHAPES

Trace three leaf templates (p. 89) onto the metal sheet. Cut out the leaves and finish the edges with files and sandpaper. Drill a hole at the top of each leaf. Stamp letters, words, phrases, or designs on each leaf.

Apply patina to the leaves. Sand the surfaces to create contrast with the stamped letters. Attach the leaves to the bottom of the hoop with 3.75mm jump rings. Tumble if desired. Attach the bail to the leather cord with the remaining three 3.75mm jump rings.

Fleuriste
cuff

Decorate a readymade cuff blank to create this cuff. You'll come across a few unusual techniques in this project, including riveting, so you may want to review all the instructions before you get started.

Chrysanthemum

Materials

For the Chrysanthemum unit:
Copper jump rings:
- 16-gauge 5mm (1)
- 21 gauge 3/32" copper rings (31)

Sterling silver jump rings:
- 21-gauge 3/32" (44)

Brass jump rings:
- 18-gauge 5/32" (11)

Single layer of thin leather, approx. 4 x 4"
Brass cuff blank, 3/4" wide
Small double-cap rivets, solid brass (5)

Tools

Chain mail/wirework toolkit
Leatherwork toolkit
Metalwork tookit:
- Annealing
- Forming

Oval bracelet mandrel
Needle file
Texture hammer
Drill with 1/4" and #59 bits
Rivet setter

The cuff components

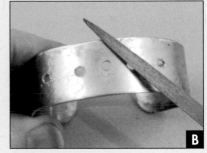

TIP
This piece may require some finessing. Gluing the leather pieces in addition to riveting allows you to cover the rivets and add additional embellishments if desired.

CHAIN MAIL
Make one Chrysanthemum unit with the copper, sterling silver, and brass jump rings [A].

BRASS CUFF
Anneal and quench the cuff blank. Place the blank on the bracelet mandrel and apply texture to the edges with a texture hammer. Using the 1/4" drill bit, drill a centered hole for placing the Chrysanthemum unit and two additional holes on each side for placing the leaves. Smooth the holes with a file [B]. The holes must be just large enough to accommodate the short, larger end of the rivet. Test each one; if necessary, rotate the drill bit in the hole with outward pressure until the rivet fits perfectly [C].

LEATHER SHAPES
Make leaf templates from scrap metal. You can use the templates shown on p. 89 or real leaves from your garden. Place the leaf template on a thin piece of leather and trim around it with your craft knife. Cut one of the leaves in

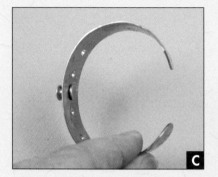

half lengthwise. Dye and finish the leather as explained in the leather tutorial, except do not glue two layers together, since a thin layer works best with this design. If desired, lightly sand the top edges to create natural-looking leaves. Use the awl to scratch veins into each leaf **[D]**.

Use the #59 drill bit to drill holes near the edge of the four whole leaves; vary the placement of the holes from leaf to leaf. This hole will need to be made larger, but rather than use a larger drill (which tends to grab and twist the leather), use a utility knife to cut around the edge of the hole until the leaf fits onto the shaft of the rivet. Do not drill a hole in the half-leaves.

CONNECTIONS

Begin attaching leaves to the cuff, starting at one side. Insert the top half of a rivet into the hole in a leaf. Insert the rivet's bottom half up through a hole in the cuff. Place the assembly on the bracelet mandrel, position the rivet setter on the rivet, and tap it with your hammer until it snaps together. Repeat to attach the remaining three whole leaves **[E]**.

Attach the Chrysanthemum unit to the center hole in the same way.

Use contact cement to secure the top leaf to the bottom leaf on each side. Place a half-leaf on each side of the Chrysanthemum unit and cement it in place to cover each rivet.

Keitaro

Akemi

Japanese

variations

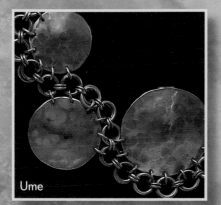

Ume

Izumo

Otobe

The Japanese category of chain mail usually consists of layers of jump rings held together by smaller rings, although you can find many complicated variations as well. This tutorial is a basic 12-in-2 pattern; it is the basis for many more-complicated weaves. The flat surface of these weaves makes Japanese-style chain a perfect foil for leather and metal shapes.

This tutorial demonstrates the 12-in-2 weave using 16 18-gauge 3.25mm jump rings (shown in antiqued brass) and 14 20-gauge 2.75mm jump rings (silver). This technique can be adapted to connect any lengths of chain made in A and B.

The most common ring sizes used for sturdy jewelry made with this type of weave are 18-gauge 3.25mm and 20-gauge 2.75mm.

Japanese Variations Tutorial

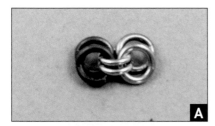

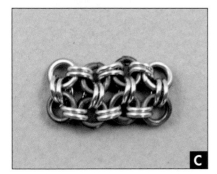

Close all the 3.25mm (large) rings and open all the 2.75mm (small) rings. Pass an open ring through four closed rings and close it. Pass another open ring through the same four closed rings. Arrange the chain in a 2+2+2 pattern **[A]**.

Add to the chain by passing a small ring through two of the previously added large rings and two new large rings. Repeat to add a second small ring through the same four large rings. Continue until the chain consists of eight pairs of large rings connected to seven pairs of small rings **[B]**.

Fold the chain in half. Pass a small ring through the two large rings on each end and close it. Pass an additional small ring through the same two pairs and close it. Repeat across the row until the chains are connected into a rectangle **[C]**.

Keitaro
choker

The weave for this choker uses four sizes of rings. The ring sizes increase slightly with each row so the chain mail flares gently outward and lies well when worn.

Japanese

Materials

Sterling silver jump rings:
- 21-gauge ³⁄₃₂" (312)
- 20-gauge ⁹⁄₆₄" (60)
- 20-gauge ⁵⁄₃₂" (60)
- 20-gauge ³⁄₁₆" (60)
- 18-gauge 3mm (3)

Sterling silver sheet, 22- or 24-gauge, about 3 x 4", to create shapes from templates

Tools

Chain mail/wirework toolkit
Metalwork toolkits:
- Cutting/filing
- Soldering
- Finishing

Dapping block (optional)

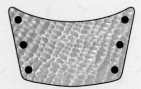

connector (make 5)

toggle loop

end piece

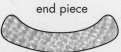

toggle bar (with soldered ring)

templates

CHAIN MAIL

Build each weave section row by row, and then connect the rows. For the first row, use four pairs of ⁹⁄₆₄" rings to connect five pairs of 21-gauge, ³⁄₃₂" rings. For the second row, use four pairs of 21-gauge, ³⁄₃₂" rings to connect five pairs of ⁵⁄₃₂" rings. For the third row, use four pairs of 21-gauge, ³⁄₃₂" rings to connect five pairs of ³⁄₁₆" rings **[A]**.

Place the three rows on your work surface. Use pairs of 21-gauge, ³⁄₃₂" rings to connect the first pair of rings in the first row to the first pair of rings in the second row, and the first pair of rings in the second row to the first pair of rings in the third row. Repeat to add connecting rings to the remaining four columns of rings to make a chain mail panel **[B]**.

Repeat the process to make a total of six chain mail panels. Antique the panels if desired.

METAL SHAPES

Prepare the shapes following the templates, adding texture and patina if desired and dapping the shapes lightly to give each shape a slight curve. Drill holes in the shapes as shown on the templates. Solder a jump ring to the underside of the toggle bar shape **[C]**.

Attach the chain mail panels to the shapes with 21-gauge, ³⁄₃₂" jump rings, placing the small rings at the top and the large rings at the bottom **[D]**. Attach one half of the toggle clasp to each end of the chain mail panel.

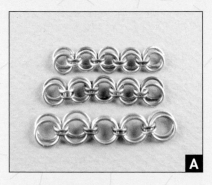

A

B

C

D

Akemi
earrings

These earrings use a simple 2+2 chain pattern. Antiqued copper and amber-colored beads give them an organic, vintage feel.

Japanese

Materials

Antiqued copper jump rings:
- 18-gauge 3.25mm copper rings (36) (large)
- 20-gauge 2.75mm copper rings (40) (small)
- 20- or 22-gauge copper sheet, approx. 2 x 2"

4–5mm top-drilled beads (10)

Antiqued copper headpins (10)

Pair of earring wires or post-back earring findings

Tools

Chain mail/wirework toolkit

Metalwork toolkits:
- Cutting/filing
- Forming

template

METALWORK

Follow the template to make two triangle shapes. Apply the texture and patina of your choice.

CHAIN MAIL

Using ten large rings and eight small, make a 2+2 chain. Using six large rings and four small, make a second, shorter 2+2 chain. Attach the shorter chain to the three middle rings of the longer chain using small rings. Attach two additional large rings to the center ring of the bottom triplet using small rings. Repeat to make a second Japanese 12-in-2 section for the other earring.

Place the chain below each triangle shape and mark placement of the holes **[A]**. Using a #67 drill bit, drill five evenly spaced holes along the bottom of each triangle and one at the top of each as shown on the template. Use a file to remove any burs and smooth the edges of the shapes.

BEAD DANGLES

Make 10 wrapped-loop dangles with the beads and headpins.

CONNECTIONS

Attach each chain mail section to a triangle using the small rings. Attach a bead dangle to each of the five bottom rings using the existing large rings **[B]**. Attach each triangle to an ear wire.

Ume
suite

The Ume suite of necklace, earrings, and bracelet has a theme of disks connected with a simple 2+2 chain. Large wire rings in place of the metal or leather disks would create an entirely different look for this wonderful Japanese variation.

Materials—earrings

Sterling silver jump rings:
- 18-gauge 3mm (large) (48)

Antiqued sterling silver jump rings:
- 20-gauge 2.5mm (small) (44)

Sterling silver disks:
- ⅝" diameter (2)
- ½" diameter (2)

Pair of earring wires or post-back earring findings

Materials for a 7" bracelet

Antiqued brass rings:
- 18-gauge 3.25mm (76)
- 20-gauge 2.75mm (125)

Finished leather disks, ¾" in diameter (7)
Antiqued brass clasp

Materials for a 17" necklace

Antiqued copper rings:
- 18-gauge 6mm (large) (126)
- 20-gauge 2.75mm (small) (124)

Copper disks, 20-gauge:
- 1¼" (large) (1)
- 1" (medium) (2)
- ¾" (small) (2)

Clasp

Tools

Chain mail/wirework toolkit
Leatherwork toolkit
Metalwork tool kits:
- Cutting/filing
- Forming
- Finishing

The earring components

The bracelet components

The necklace components

EARRINGS
CHAIN MAIL

Make a 2+2+2 chain, starting with a pair of large rings and alternating with small rings until the chain is 13 pairs of large rings long. Repeat to make a second chain of the same length.

STERLING SILVER DISKS

Add patina and texture to the disks as desired. Dap and finish the disks.

CONNECTIONS

Using the chain as a guide, mark and drill six evenly spaced holes in the small disk and nine evenly spaced holes in the large disk to link the disks to the chain as shown in the main photo on p. 103. Attach the chain to the disks using a single small ring through pairs of large rings in the chain. (Two pairs of medium rings will be attached to both disks.) Attach an earring wire above the large disk, passing it through the second pair of large rings.

Repeat to make a second earring, but reverse the placement of the large and small disks so the second earring mirrors the first.

You can purchase metal disks, use a disk cutter to cut them from a sheet of fairly thin-gauge metal, or use a template to draw them and a saw or metal shears to cut them out. The texture in the earrings was made using a well-worn utility hammer; I used the ball end of a chasing hammer to texture the disks used in the necklace.

BRACELET
CHAIN MAIL

Alternating both ring sizes, make a 2+2 chain that has 38 pairs of large rings.

LEATHER SHAPES

Make seven leather disks and finish as desired. Using the chain for placement, and drill seven evenly spaced holes in each disk.

CONNECTIONS

Attach the 2+2 chain to the disks using 2.75mm jump rings, following the photo on p. 103. Attach half of the clasp to each end pair of jump rings with a 2.75mm jump ring.

NECKLACE
CHAIN MAIL

Make a 2+2 chain, alternating pairs of large and small rings, until the chain is the desired length.

COPPER DISKS

Apply texture and patina to the disks **[A]**. Finish the edges. Use a dapping block and punch to dome the disks slightly **[B]**.

Using the chain for placement, mark and drill nine evenly spaced holes in the large disk. Mark and drill six holes in each of the remaining disks **[C]**.

CONNECTIONS

Following the photo on p. 103, work from the center outward to attach the chain to the disks using small rings. Use 18-gauge rings to attach half of the clasp to each necklace end.

TIP
As you prepare the leather for the bracelet, it's a good idea to make extra disks in case of a mistake or to lengthen the bracelet.

Izumo
bracelet

The Izumo Bracelet uses a traditional Japanese 12-in-2 weave attached to leather squares. The leather colors and techniques available give you many design alternatives. Use school colors, a sports charm, and jersey numbers, and you'll have a school spirit bracelet.

Japanese

Materials
Sterling silver jump rings:
- 18-gauge 3.25mm (large) (72)
- 20-gauge 2.75mm (small) (88)
- 18-gauge 3.0mm (2)

Finished leather shapes, ¾" square (5)
Silver-colored ball-and-socket clasp

Tools
Chain mail toolkit
Leatherwork toolkit

The bracelet components

CHAIN MAIL
Using twelve large rings and eight small rings, make two 2+2 chains. Place the chains next to each other and connect them by using the small ring pairs to link the large ring pairs. Repeat to make three additional sections. Make two triangles by attaching a three-large-ring chain to a two-large-ring chain and a single pair of large rings to the two-large-ring chain.

LEATHER SHAPES
Make the leather squares in the desired color and finish. Place the chain next to the leather squares to determine hole placement. Drill three evenly spaced holes on two opposing sides of each leather square.

CONNECTIONS
Use the small rings to connect the chain sections to the leather squares. Attach a chain triangle to each bracelet end using small jump rings. Attach half of the clasp to the point of each triangle using 18-gauge 3.0mm jump rings.

Otobe
necklace

The Otobe necklace is another example
of how chain mail can be used in a
supporting role. In this design, the metal
element has equal status. The cloud shape
would look beautiful in leather as well.

Japanese

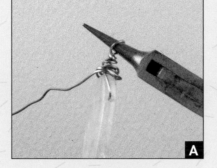

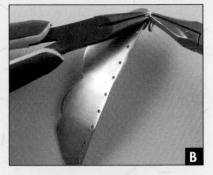

Materials

Copper jump rings:
- 18-gauge 3.50mm copper rings (large) (50)
- 18-gauge 3.25mm copper rings (medium) (144) for 2+2 chain
- 20-gauge 2.75mm copper rings (small) (202)

Copper sheet, 20- or 22-gauge, approx. 2 x 5"
4–5mm side-drilled beads (8)
30mm top-drilled bead
40" 24- or 26-gauge copper wire
Clasp

Tools

Chain mail toolkit
Leatherwork toolkit
Metalwork toolkits:
- Cutting/filing
- Forming
- Finishing

METAL SHAPES

Saw out the cloud shape as shown in the template, and finish with the texture and patina of your choice. Curve the shape slightly using your fingers or a bracelet mandrel and a rawhide mallet. Mark and drill 10 evenly spaced holes at the bottom and two at the top as shown on the template.

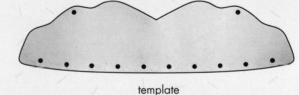

template

CHAIN MAIL

Using 20 large rings and 18 small, make a 2+2 chain that is 10-large-ring pairs long. Using 16 large rings and 14 small, make a 2+2 chain that is eight-large-ring pairs long. Using four large rings and two small rings, make a 2+2 chain. Make another 2+2 chain. Set aside six closed large rings and six open small rings.

BEAD DANGLES

Using about 8" of copper wire, make a wrapped-loop dangle with the large bead, coiling the wire down and around the bead in a loose, irregular wrap [A]. Use about 4" of wire to wrap the small beads in the same way. Antique all of the components if desired.

CONNECTIONS

Slide a small ring into each hole in the bottom of the cloud shape [B] and use it to attach the 10-large-ring chain. Starting at the left side of the first chain (row 1), attach the eight-large-ring chain using the small rings. To the eight-large-ring chain: Attach a 2+2 chain to the row-2 ring pair and another 2+2 chain to the row-7 ring pair from the right. Attach a ring pair in rows 3, 8, and 10. Connect the 10-ring chain to the sheet metal cloud shape using small jump rings [C]. Attach small-bead dangles to the bottom pairs of rings in rows 1–4 and 7–10. Attach the large-bead dangle to the two bottom pairs of rings in rows 5 and 6. Use an 18-gauge ring to attach one end of each long chain to the top holes in the shape [D]. Use an 18-gauge ring to attach half of the clasp to the other end of each chain.

About the Author

Resources

As you begin to explore the unconventional style of chain mail, I suggest you start with your local suppliers of beads, metal, and leather. Online sources are great for locating specialty items or particular sizes of jump rings. The suppliers listed here are just a starting point.

Rio Grande
riogrande.com
Metal, tools, findings, just about anything

B. Craus
bcraus.com
Tools, hand-engraved texture hammers, metals, and stamps

Herkimer Diamond Mine
herkimerdiamond.com
Herkimer diamonds of all sizes

C&T Designs
candtdesigns.com
Perfect pre-cut jump rings and custom cuts

Potter USA
potterusa.com
Ring-cutting tools and saw blades

Beads of Cambay
beadsofcambay.com
Quality gemstones

Tandy Leather
tandyleather.com
Everything for leatherwork

Turtle Feathers
turtlefeathers.net
Leather paints, dyes—even glitter!

Laura Poplin loves to spread the joy of chain mail by teaching others, and has taught classes in various venues in the Dayton, Ohio, area. A special passion for her is working with developmentally disabled people and helping them discover their artistic abilities through making jewelry.

Laura's jewelry line, *"enchaînements,"* is shown at several Dayton-area galleries and boutiques and on her website, laurapoplin.com. She was a finalist in the 2010 Halstead Grand Competition for up-and-coming jewelry business entrepreneurs. She is a member of the Ohio Arts Council, the Dayton Visual Arts Center, and the American Craft Council.

Acknowledgments

Many people have been a part of the linking of scenes and of ideas that led to me to write this book. Thanks to:

Mary Wohlgemuth, my editor, for discovering my work, having the idea, and for being the major link—the one who soldered and wrapped it all into existence.

Mary Lou Craft for inviting me to the first chain mail class that led me to discover my passion for creating unconventional chain mail jewelry.

Pat Antonick for being the first person to encourage me to sell my work and cheering me on ever since.

The Dayton Visual Arts Center for being the catalyst for many Ohio artists, including me, to first experience selling their artwork.

Ray Gooch of Mystic Leather, who taught me the basics of leatherwork.

Kathleen Kargl, Adjunct Professor at the University of Dayton, and graphic designers Kathryn Sturm and Lauren Graehler.

The Mail Artisans International League, my go-to place for information and problem solving.

These encouraging people: Kathy Weaver, Lenie Vessey, Charlene Sparks, Glenda Swartz, Bonnie Rizzo, Loretta Puncer (artist and owner of the Gallery 510), Larry Ellis, and Monique Barnhart.

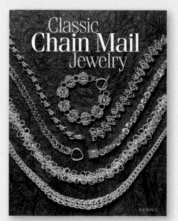